"*Savage Gods* is a beautiful, intelligent, extremely poetic book about a writer dissecting his thoughts and feelings on the page without the protective layer of fiction."
—**Gabino Iglesias, NPR**

"The most incredible book I read this year… Kingsnorth charts the breakdown of his faith in words, in nature as an uncomplicated restorative, in the idea of 'progress', while fearlessly tracking his conclusions to their very ends. This is a writer—and a writer that burns—attempting to cure himself of writing, on the page, and it leads to some profound, and just as often jaw-dropping, insights."
—**David Keenan, *The Guardian***

"A success… [Paul Kingsnorth] is a man bearing everything. And for all the confessional memoirs so popular at the moment, this is the real deal."
—**Scott Beauchamp, *The American Conservative***

"*Savage Gods* is a compromise of a book, too, veering between inner and outer worlds, shape-shifting from narrative to aphorism to vision. But tidiness is indisposed to containing multitudes, and there's a price to pay in retaining them. Kingsnorth's troublesome words do an unexpectedly moving job of capturing the problem of being, and of writing about it."
—**Nina Lyon, *The Spectator***

"Like all the best books, [*Savage Gods* is] a wail sent up from the heart of one of the intractable problems of the human condition: real change comes only from crisis, and crisis always involves loss… There are few writers as raw or brave on the page. *Savage Gods* is an important book."
—**Ellie Robins, *Los Angeles Review of Books***

"Paul Kingsnorth has always held my attention, and at times completely astounded me with his varied and vital writing talent. This spectacular little volume is a book all about that writing talent, but discussions of process and craft are secondary to a more ontological exploration of what writing really is... and what it very much isn't."
—**Mark Schultz, Carmichael's Bookstore**

"A sprawling meditation stuffed to the gills with poetry and literature. Kingsnorth looks at the decisions that made his life, roads taken and not. 'If not writing, then what?' he asks. Then what, indeed. All I can say is that I'm glad Kingsnorth has answered with this lovely book, full of wisdom."
—**Spencer Ruchti, Harvard Bookstore**

"Paul Kingsnorth is one of my favorite writers and thinkers out there today. In *Savage Gods*, his deeply personal musings on writing and its value (or even relevance) in the face of global and environmental crises are heartfelt and thought-provoking."
—**Chris La Tray, Fact & Fiction Bookstore**

"*Savage Gods* is a deeply personal memoir of the ecology of home and an unusual and frank account of a writer's experience."
—**Melanie Challenger, author of *On Extinction***

"Horrible and brilliant and terribly important. This book is what I've been looking for for years, and what I'd hoped never to see."
—**Charles Foster, author of *Being A Beast***

"A poignant, honest portrait of a crisis of faith, not in God or Self but a far rarer thing, a crisis of belief in words themselves, the very materials of the writer's mind."
—**Jay Griffiths, author of *Wild***

Also by Paul Kingsnorth

NON-FICTION

One No, Many Yeses

Real England

Uncivilisation: the Dark Mountain Manifesto
(with Dougald Hine)

Confessions of a Recovering Environmentalist

FICTION

The Wake

Beast

Alexandria

POETRY

Kidland and other poems

Songs from the Blue River

SAVAGE GODS

PAUL KINGSNORTH

Two Dollar Radio
Books too loud to Ignore

Two Dollar Radio
Books too loud to Ignore

WHO WE ARE
Two Dollar Radio is a family-run outfit dedicated to reaffirming the cultural and artistic spirit of the publishing industry. We aim to do this by presenting bold works of literary merit, each book, individually and collectively, providing a sonic progression that we believe to be too loud to ignore.

TwoDollarRadio.com

Proudly based in
Columbus
OHIO

 @TwoDollarRadio

   @TwoDollarRadio

 /TwoDollarRadio

This book was manufactured using responsibly sourced paper.

PRINTED IN THE U.S.A.

SOME RECOMMENDED LOCATIONS FOR READING *SAVAGE GODS*:
Pretty much anywhere because books are portable and the perfect technology!

AUTHOR PHOTO→
Clare McNamee

COVER ARTWORK→
Two Dollar Radio

Two Dollar Radio would like to acknowledge that the land where we live and work is the contemporary territory of multiple Indigenous Nations.

If only we arrange our life in accordance with the principle which tells us that we must always trust in the difficult, then what now appears to us as the most alien will become our most intimate and trusted experience. How could we forget those ancient myths that stand at the beginning of all races, the myths about dragons that at the last moment are transformed into princesses? Perhaps all the dragons in our lives are princesses who are only waiting to see us act, just once, with beauty and courage.

Rilke

There's more to life than books, you know,
but not much more.

The Smiths

SAVAGE GODS

Writers are lost people.

Nobody would write a book if they weren't lost. Nobody would write a book if they were not in search of paradise, and nobody would be in search of paradise unless they believed it might exist somewhere, which means *out there*, which means *just beyond my reach*. Writers can see paradise, but can never touch it. Writers want to belong to a place that is just beyond their reach, because if they were to reach the place they would have to do the hard work of being in it. Writers don't belong anywhere, or to anyone, and they do not want to. They are driven by some severance and none of them understands it. Not just writers. Painters. Musicians. Artists. Art is the search for intact things in a world in which all things are broken.

That paragraph was dishonest. I am going to rewrite it.

Here goes.

I am a lost person. I wouldn't write books if I wasn't lost. I wouldn't write anything at all if I wasn't in search of paradise, and I wouldn't be in search of paradise if I didn't need it; if I didn't think I would be less lost if I were to find it. So I write to find it... but no, not that either, because I am nearing middle-age now and I know there is nothing to find. I know now that my paradise is not in a cave on a South Sea island or in the montane rainforests of Borneo where the gibbons call or in a *finca* in Patagonia or down the side streets of Mexico City, in a blue house with yellow doors and shutters that the sun comes through and wakes me, and orange trees. There is no paradise out there, so I write to create my paradise on paper or on this blank, flat screen, but something in me always sabotages it and turns it dark. So then I write to reorder the world so that paradise might look possible again even for a moment, for someone. I don't belong anywhere, or to anyone. I am driven by some severance and I don't understand it.

That's better.

I am sitting in a field in the west of Ireland. It is a long, thin field, grass and dock and plantain and ground ivy, hedged in with thorn and sycamore and elder. The air is primaveral. The field is impacted with thin plastic coils, each about two feet long, pointing up to the sky, about a hundred of them. It's as if something up there has been throwing darts at me. I sit among the coils. Each one encloses a young tree which I planted this winter with my wife and my two young children. This is our field.

I thought that if I had a field then I would feel less lost. I thought that if I had some land I would belong somewhere. And sometimes I feel it has started to happen. Sometimes I think the place is looking out at me, curious. *He's been here for a while. What's he up to?* Other times I sit in the field, in the circle of Scots pines we have planted on the highest point and I feel I am not here at all. This is my field, but it doesn't feel like mine. What could it ever feel like to *own* a piece of ground? I have never felt like I really owned anything. If you don't believe you really exist, you can't believe you own anything. Sometimes I can sit in the field, like I am sitting here now, and feel like I am floating on air and through it and on into empty space.

2.

This field: it belongs to us, to me and my wife, because we paid for it and we have a piece of paper lodged with a lawyer somewhere that proves it. But my lifetime will flicker out and this field will still be here, as it was before I came. I am passing through this field like the heron sometimes passes above it and foxes come through every night and red-tailed bumbles drone past on their way to the hedgebank petals. I am here now, and then I will be gone again.

So the field does not belong to me, really. Do I belong to the field? Probably not that either. I would like to. But I have only been on this land for three years. I have only been in the country for three years. I am a blow-in, as we are called in these parts. You can't just turn up in a place and claim it. A place needs to claim you. People belong across two axes: time and space. My neighbors' names are on the tombstones 'round here, and mine is not. How much does that matter? It is not everything, I think, but neither is it nothing. Money whips us around like a tornado, money and capital, greed and ambition and hunger and power, they uproot people and scatter them about and we all keep our heads down as the Machine passes through, drizzling us across the landscapes of the world, breaking the link between people and place and time, demanding our labor and our gratitude, hypnotizing us with its white light, transforming us into eaters, consumers of experience and consumers of place, players of games, servants.

Is displacement good? Is it good to be lost and far from home, even if you are still at home? Are we all lost and far from home? I think I could build an argument around that. I think the world is lost and far from home, and that all the people flooding across borders everywhere, from village to city, from country to country, fleeing the hardship or chasing the money, dug up by the Machine and dumped on the concrete, working to keep the wheels turning and to keep us all from being able to belong anywhere ever again—well, what do I think about that? What do I think, really?

No. I am going to avoid building any arguments. I am going to refuse to stake a claim, to build a case and then defend it. The minute you circle the wagons you are vulnerable. What if you didn't even want to defend that territory? What if it was not worth dying for? Everyone is picking fights out there. In the streets at night, on the feeds when they should be working, in 140 characters with borrowed opinions and impossible levels of anger. I can't do it, not anymore. It's all wasted energy, the flaring of a billion daytime candles. Why light them? What do they illuminate?

I felt far from home even when I was young and at home. Now I have come to a foreign country to make a new home because I could not make a home in my own country, because in my own country a small house and a field is beyond the means of anyone who does not earn a lot of money or who refuses to get into debt to chase a dream. I think there is something wrong with this. But I like being here, and now, if I go back to my home country I miss my new home. I feel that something in this new home—the place itself, the work we have put in, the trees we have planted—is softly calling me back.

Sometimes.

But there are other times, and I have only recently allowed myself to really see them. These other times, I think to myself: I came here to belong somewhere. I came here, at last, to have a home. I wandered the world driven by this severance, thinking I needed a home, thinking that the work of being in a place would still my unquiet mind. Now I have a home, and I like it. I like planting trees, building walls, collecting eggs from my hens. I like scything down the grass and pitchforking the hay. I like splitting logs, I like the sunset over the field, I like the silence and the birdsong. I like building up, slowly, a wildlife haven and a family haven. I would rather be here than anywhere else. I appreciate the gift of it.

But my mind, and the fire that was long ago set beneath, it remains unquiet. There is some small, insistent animal in me, still restless. Did I tell myself that life was a climb up steep cliffs to a green plateau, and is it not that? Did I think that being here would be enough? What if it isn't enough? What if I want to belong precisely because I can't? What if the things I thought were anchoring me were only stories, which blow away when the wind changes? What happens when the wind changes? What happens when the animal escapes?

What happens when your stories don't work anymore? Your words?

3.

I had a plan. I always have a plan. Without a plan, I am lost and fumbling. It's a skill, making plans like this, containing your life and direction within them, a skill that can get you to places you always wanted to be, a skill that can get you out ahead of others who don't have plans, who don't have a direction. *Ha ha*, you think, as you sail by, *look at me! Look at my plan! I am in control of my life! I know how to sail!* Usually you think this right before you hit a squall and end up in the sea, clinging to a plank of splintered wood. You are not as good a sailor as you thought you were.

That's the trap. A plan can become, in an eye-blink, a cage arrayed around you like swords in a tarot deck. Sometimes you find that your plan is so good that you can't escape from it. You get to where you wanted to be, and there is nothing else there. Only you, suddenly lonely and with no way back. I inherited my compulsion for plan-making from my father, whose need for control eventually killed him, so I should really have learned my lesson. But lessons don't work like that, do they? Not for me, anyway. I don't think I have ever learned a lesson in my life. I don't watch somebody make a mistake and conclude, *well, I'll make sure I don't do that, then.* We pretend that we can learn lessons like this because the alternative is to face the music: to accept that most of what we do in our human lives is driven by some deep, old compulsion we can neither understand nor control, and that when it comes upon us, all we can do is hold on to the wrecked boat and pray. Or laugh, depending on our personalities.

I had a plan. The plan was to settle, to have some land, to root myself and my family. To escape from the city, to escape from the traps. To grow our own food, educate our own kids, draw our own water, plant our own fuel. To be closer to nature and further from the Machine. To be freer, to be more in control. To escape and, at the same time, to belong. To learn things I didn't know anything about but wanted to, because I felt they'd make me a better, rounder adult person: planting trees, keeping hens, managing woodland, carpentry, wiring, building, all the small skills required to run a few acres of land and to be part of it. On top of that, to bring up our young children at home. And on top of that, to write books: truer books than I had ever written before. To write something great, something real, something so intense that nobody could read it without dimming the lights first.

It's good to be ambitious. Or is it? I don't even know anymore.

We—my wife, myself, our two young children—moved to this small townland in Ireland when I was 41 years old. Our house is on a small rise, on good sandy loam, a few miles from the River Shannon, which divides the east of this island from the west. We are in the west of the country, just, which means we are in the Romantic bit. The house is a little two-bedroom concrete cottage—can you have a concrete cottage?—built—poured—in the 1950s, to replace an older stone-and-thatch affair. The history of Ireland is a history of people escaping just as soon as they could from the tiny, picturesque, damp, cramped, whitewash-and-thatch cottages which people from the rest of the world still associate with Ireland.

Our house is small and a bit damp. It is not surrounded by breathtaking mountain scenery or sweeping white beaches, because we could never afford to live anywhere like that. It is quite an ordinary little place—modest compared to many new rural homes—which suits me somehow, because I feel I am quite an ordinary person, and I could never live in a big house. The land around it is gentle: crooked fields, still owned by small farmers, home to beef cows, a few sheep, the odd goat, and occasionally a strip of wheat or barley. The fields are divided by hedges of thorn, elder, oak, ash, sycamore, lime, under which streams run and past which old lanes wind. It is a pleasant, unspectacular, nooky, modest sort of landscape. It is my home, though I am still a stranger in it.

We moved here from a small Cumbrian market town where we had lived for five years, though I'm not from there either. Where am I from? I was born in Worcester, lived in Malvern until I was two or three—I don't remember it—then moved to the suburbs of northwest London, near to where both my parents had grown up. When I was 11 we moved to High Wycombe, an ugly town in Buckinghamshire which had been an attractive town in Buckinghamshire before the 1960s got hold of it. Then we moved to a small village near Bath, in the west country, the kind of village with no farmers left in it. When I was 18 I went to university in Oxford. Then I moved to London. Then back to Oxford. Then to Cumbria. Now to Ireland. Meanwhile, my parents had moved to Surrey, then to Cyprus where my nan, a Greek Cypriot from Famagusta, had met my granddad in the war. When my dad died in Cyprus, my mum moved back to England: to Yorkshire, then to Cheshire. My two brothers are currently in Reading and Warrington. We're not done yet. See how we run.

My wife, Jyoti, had it different. She was born in Darlington, but from a young age she lived in Leamington Spa, in the same 1930s semi where her mum still lives. Her mum is a Punjabi Sikh, as was her late father and gran. The family moved from India to Britain in the late 1960s, invited by the government to plug the gaps in the British labor market; a fair exchange for a few centuries of colonialism. We occupied your country—now come and drive our buses! Jyoti's family moved across half a world, but now they're more settled than I am. She still has a family home. I wish I had a family home. I can remember when I had one. I couldn't wait to get away.

4.

My plan went wrong almost immediately. When I first arrived here, instead of feeling liberated, I felt like crying. I had loved the little town we lived in, where my son was born, where my daughter went to school, where I joined the fell running club and labored up and down mountains every Tuesday night then went to some small rural pub for sausages and beer. I had felt more at home there than at any time in my adult life. I wrote my first novel there, which I could afford to do because Jyoti was a psychiatrist who earned actual money. But psychiatry was killing her, her role was not to cure people but to medicate them, to stick plasters on the wounds the Machine had gouged into the people at the bottom of the pile. There was nothing she could do about the wounds, and they kept coming. We had always talked about owning some land, moving to a smallholding. Jyoti thought about her mum's village in India, where her mum had tamed a wild mynah bird, where her granddad was the village wise man, where her gran milked the family buffalo, where there were bombardments of morning birdsong that would wake you from your sleep on the flat roof. I thought of little farms I had seen and camped in on long walks with my dad over the hills of Britain as a child and how they represented something to me that was very different from the flatness of the suburbs. I thought about sheepdogs and hens and lambs and the still of the tangled banks. The green stillness. In Cumbria, only the rich can afford their patch of the green stillness.

We left Cumbria because we weren't millionaires, but we also left because I was driven by my severance, my lifelong companion, and I needed to push away, as far away as I could push from everything I had known. I was getting complacent. I was starting to *enjoy myself.* I had friends and hobbies and a hometown

I liked and this was intolerable. I could see myself getting fat and cozy and staying in the same place forever and this vision filled me with horror. I had to go because I was starting to get comfortable, and I have always run from things—houses, towns, jobs, girlfriends—when they started to make me feel comfortable. Until I was 35, I ran away from being at home, and then I wanted to be at home. Don't ask me to explain this. How would I know how to explain it? I'm a writer, not a therapist.

5.

Maybe that does explain it. I'm a writer, and to me this has always been a calling, a duty. It has always been my guiding light, my personal mythology. I have built my life around it: what the writing needs, the writing gets, and all else is secondary. Maybe this sounds pretentious or affected, but I can't help that. It's what I've believed and cleaved to for longer than I can remember. *I am a writer.* Writing has controlled me and now perhaps it has become me. Writing has been put, always, before everything else, because if you don't pay obeisance to the god then the god will abandon you.

And so I have always run, or so I've told myself, because the writing needed me to. The writing needed me to stay on the edge, to stay burning, to stay ahead. The writing needed me, at some level, always to be *unhappy*. If I settled anywhere and got too comfortable, I would soften around the edges and the fire would die. I would end up writing bland memoirs or ghost-written books about cats. 'You must stay drunk on writing,' advises Ray Bradbury, 'so that reality cannot destroy you.' Alice Thomson goes further, saying art that doesn't come from pain is just entertainment.

Pain, severance: it took me so long to realize their importance, their inevitability, their necessity. The grinding wheels of opposition are where the words are milled. The creation comes from the pain of the grinding. It is the heart being ground. It is the longing that creates the art, or the attempt at art. For that to happen, you need always to not quite be who, or where, you are. You need always to be under pressure, like a layer of sedimentary rock or a steel girder holding up a skyscraper. From the pressure, from the pain of the contradictions you carry and embody, from the wrenching of the oppositions that tear you, comes the energy that bursts into words, comes the flood, comes the pouring. You must always be not quite where you want to be, and you must never quite know where you want to be, and nothing must ever be enough to bring you contentment. Contentment is your deadliest foe. The fruit must always be just out of reach, and the world you walk through must always be a shade greyer than the one you can make yourself from what lives hidden in your heart.

In your multiplicity, in your contradictions, in the pulsing thrum of all your wanting and all your loss is your chance to make something that might *matter*; is your chance to capture the pure, intense moment, in all its light and rage, as if time were cast away from it forever.

6.

These are the people that I am. I want to sit with my tribe around a fire for all eternity, telling the stories my ancestors told as they listen over my shoulder, feeling at home, among my people, comforted. In the precise same moment of time I want to sit up on the mountain, looking down discontentedly at all these idiots around the fire, irritated by their stupid, comfortable complacency. I want to sit always outside the ring of people and observe them, alone. That's what writers do: we sit outside and we observe, alone. It is not a choice, and there is nothing to be done about it.

I want to do all of these things at once—be a called writer, be a rooted family man, be a tribal elder, be an outcast shaman—and this is ludicrous, impossible. *Art that doesn't come from pain is just entertainment.* And what does that mean for a man with a young family and three acres of land, a man with responsibilities and a burden of ideas in his head which he has just realized do not serve him anymore, and may not do so again?

7.

For five years or more, Jyoti and I talked about where to go. I favored the extremes: Chilean Patagonia, the French Pyrenees, Romania. The writer was pulling me, kicking me, playing with me, I think now, though it didn't occur to me then. I only knew that something in me wanted to be thrown onto the rocks, utterly alien, far from the world I knew. Jyoti, without saying much, had other ideas. She knew the gulf between my desires and what I'm actually capable of. Ireland, though, seemed workable. We had friends there, we liked it. It was across the sea, but practically so. It was still an adventure, and a new start. We could afford it, just. I worried that it wasn't radical enough, but time was pressing. Time is always pressing. Nothing presses harder, or is so relentless, so unforgiving.

So I wrenched myself away and when I got here, I wanted to cry. I had thought I felt like this for a few weeks, but Jyoti recently informed me that it was more like a year. I was angry with myself for running, for breaking what I had had. Maybe it had been necessary, but that didn't make it painless. I was English; I had always lived in England. It was my home, it was where I came from, and I was attached to it. This was an unfashionable attitude, but what was I supposed to do about that? I'd even written a book about that attachment, and yet I was still surprised to find that, when I left it to move abroad, my insides felt wrenched. Suddenly I felt I had made a terrible mistake. I felt homesick. This wasn't my place. I didn't belong here. What was I doing? I was a fucking idiot! This would not be the first time that my Romantic dreams had screwed up my life, and those of others around me, but it might end up being the most serious.

Something I'd been writing about for years, in that book and elsewhere: human cultures come from places. They arise from them, curl out of them like smoke from hot ash. People do too. We're not free actors. We can't just skip from peak to peak, buzz from city to city with no consequences. I knew this, so why didn't I *know* it? Cultures come from places. My culture comes, most recently, from the southeastern suburbs of England. It's a culture of hard work, of 'getting on,' of English Protestantism channeled into secular ambition. It's about settling down and having a family, contributing, progressing, climbing up; not bad things, necessarily, not for a lot of people. But it's also about selling up, moving on, about property ladders and career ladders, about staking your place on the consumer travelator that represents progress in a burning world. It's about feeding the Machine that rips up the people and rips up the places and turns them all against each other while the money funnels upwards to the people who are paying attention. This is the crap our children are learning. There is not much sign at all that the tide is turning.

There's a story I've told a lot in recent years. I told it in my first book, which was written 15 years ago, and then I forgot about it. Recently, though, it has returned to me, and has been hovering about. It wants something, I think.

It's a simple story. I was in the Highlands of West Papua, in New Guinea. I was 29 years old and had snuck into the country undercover, disguised as a tourist, because journalism was prohibited and I didn't want to spend time in an Indonesian jail. West Papua was—still is—occupied by the Indonesian military, and its tribal people and culture are being systematically wiped out and replaced with the culture of its mostly Javanese occupiers. I was spending time with people from the Lani Tribe, who were telling me stories of military executions, corporate land theft, the destruction of the forests by loggers, and the poisoning of the rivers by gold mines.

Three or four men were walking me through the mountain forests from one tiny collection of thatched huts to another. We were going to meet someone who could tell us stories about what the military had been doing beyond the world's gaze. The men walked in front of me, spears over their shoulders, occasionally pointing out the call of a bird-of-paradise or offering to scramble up the trees and catch one for me. ('Good feathers!' one explained, as I tried not to look horrified.) Then we reached a break in the trees. Looking out through the gap, I could see a great sweep of ancient forest rolling off towards the blue horizon. Green, blue: there was nothing else. Everything could have been here at the Creation.

The men lined up, then, with their spears over their shoulders and they sang, in a language I would never know, a song of thanks to the forest. It was all very matter-of-fact. They didn't do it for show, they didn't explain it to me—I had to ask them later what had happened—and when they had finished we just kept walking. That song must have sat within me for years until I was really ready to hear it. Only recently have I rediscovered it and started to examine it.

What does that incident carry for me? Only this: some sense of reciprocity between a people and the place they live in. Some sense of belonging. That first book of mine, written when I was a young, fiery activist, dedicated to bringing down global capitalism and ushering in a regime of worldwide economic justice—it turned out to be a little misleading in the end. It was supposed to be a travelogue, a series of visits to the heartlands of resistance to economic globalization. But I kept moving the goalposts, widening my search so that I had an excuse to spend time with people like the Papuans, or landless Brazilian farmers, or Indigenous people in southern Mexico. The middle-class Europeans blockading summits and waffling about Negri and Fanon bored me to tears. They were rootless; they were as lost as me. They came in by plane or train from some other European city, they put on their black masks and Palestinian scarves, shouted at some fat cats, got tear-gassed and then went home. Empty gestures, empty words, and I was empty too. But in the Baliem Valley in Papua or the Lacandon jungle in Mexico I found something else; something older, deeper, calmer and very much more real. I found people who *belonged* to a place. I had never seen this before. Where I grew up, there was nothing like it. It had—it still has—more meaning to me than any other way of human living I had seen. I wanted to know: what would that be like? And could I have it?

8

My family is from the lower middle class, the most derided class in England. Not callus-handed and romantically oppressed like the working class. Not classy or rich like the gentry or the aristos. Not possessed of degrees or home libraries or big wine glasses like the *haute bourgeoisie*. Not exotic and in need of stout liberal defence like the migrants. We are the class snickered at in Roald Dahl books. We come from suburbs and have family cars and watch the telly in the lounge and live in medium-sized towns in unfashionable places and have never been to the theatre and regard the *Daily Mail* as a good newspaper. I'm not speaking personally. I don't regard the *Daily Mail* as a good newspaper, though I do think it has quite a fetching logo.

And anyway, I escaped. My great grandparents were policemen, housewives, snipers on the Somme, union men, Methodists, proper old inter-war socialists in cardigans who lived in tiny terraces with outside loos and never touched a drop. My grandparents were shopkeepers, postmen, train and bus drivers, immigrant workers in camera factories, members of reserved trades, weekend coarse fishermen, allotment gardeners, rosette-winning attenders of dog shows. My dad left school at 16, became an engineer's apprentice, and set out to prove his own dad wrong. My mum met him at school, left at the same age, became a comptometer operator (look it up), then a school classroom assistant, a housewife, our mum, the still point in a not-often-still home.

Me? I'm an Oxford University graduate who writes books for a living. Look! I've worked in the jungles of Borneo and the villages of Mexico. I've done book tours of Australia and the USA. I don't have any money, but I have—no, I had—my father's ambition and I know how to look like I'm one of *them*. You know: one of the kinds of people who also have all these things but who somehow, unlike me, feel they have them by right. Who grew into them, or who always had them, or who grew up surrounded by people who did. At Oxford I would see these 19-year-old boys in tweed jackets, who wandered about full of louche, angular confidence, and they didn't seem any smarter than me but they seemed a lot more sure of themselves. I knew nothing about the world, or myself, or how to behave, and I didn't know what I was doing there, or anywhere else. But they did. They were all confident, while I was not. At least I thought they were. Now that I write this, I realize I'm not so sure. Maybe they were looking at me the same way. Where did this chip on my shoulder fall from? I think my dad must have dropped it as he was passing. It's not attractive. I wonder if I will pass it on to my children. I am trying not to.

This is me: a wanderer through words and through the world. A wanderer who is often sick of wandering, who is not a natural at this, who wants to put down roots, or feels he would be a better and more whole and more productive member of society if he did, and who was brought up that way. At the same time I am someone whose soul drifts like a cloudbank, someone who feels sick at the very notion of being productive, someone who wants to be anything but a member of society, thinks society stinks and has nothing to do with him. There is the battle, maybe within us all. The West battles the East, the old battles the new, modernity battles tradition, inside all of us, all of the time. It's exhausting, don't you find?

This is the battle I have used my words to document for so many years. Now, suddenly, something is happening that I never expected or prepared for. All the words are dropping away.

9.

Three years ago, I arrived here, in my new green stillness, in a land that had been stripped bare for centuries by people from my land, and I started to fragment. I felt like I was falling apart. After the first few weeks, the initial anxiety dissipated, but I still felt the scales dropping off my skin one by one. All of my comfortable certainties looked less comfortable. Surrounded now by people of different origins, classes, ages, backgrounds, I saw more clearly than ever that for most of my adult life I had been hanging about with people like myself: middle-class graduates, liberal-leftish, urban, left-brained, intellectual, floating, disconnected. That stuff wouldn't wash here. Suddenly it all seemed painfully self-conscious and individualist, and so did I. In the city, in the town even, there was no real need to talk to your neighbors if you didn't want to. I had never really learned how to do it properly; I was not good at talking to people at the best of times, which was probably another reason I had become a writer. But out here, everybody knew your business, especially if you were a blow-in like me. You had to talk to your neighbors, and they felt like neighbors, not just people who happened to be living in the next house along for now, before they moved on to something and somewhere better.

The position I had painfully staked out in the world began to fragment. I began to fragment. I am still fragmenting, I think. Sometimes it scares me, sometimes it excites me. You have to come apart to be put back together in a different shape. You have to be reformed, or you rust up, and all your parts stop moving.

Soon enough, my writing began to fragment too, because the kind of words you create to speak to the urban crowds of the alienated West don't come from places like this. This old land out in the west, this ground will not give you what you need in that regard. It has no intention of helping. I mean that. I think, more and more, that words come from places, that they seep up into you and that places like this will not give words to people like me that speak to the things I used to be and used to believe. The words that come from this place, that bubble up from it, don't even always make sense to me. I don't know what they are trying to say or what they want. But they want something, and it is not what I once thought I came here to do. All I know right now is that my words don't work the way they used to. I used to think words were my tools. Now I think it might be the other way around.

I wonder what they want me to make.

What does a writer do when his words stop working? I don't know. All I know is that I am churning inside and everything I knew is windskipping like brown willow leaves in a winter gale. I am afraid and sometimes I am excited. I feel like something is waiting for me, and I don't know what, but I fear that I do know. I fear that I am being called, and I am taking too long to answer. But who is to say how long it should take?

I don't know. I don't know much at the moment. It feels like all the things I was so sure about have dissolved away from me. I don't even know who I am now. When I came here, I thought I would at least know *where* I am, but that, too, the longer I look at it, turns out not to be quite true either. The more I look at anything, the more questions I seem to have about it. All the stories I had are dissolving away. None of the scaffolding holds.

All the words I used to have: once they would have closed these paragraphs comfortably on the page. Almost without me thinking about it, they would have offered up a well-wrought conclusion, a rallying cry. They would have rounded-off, tied up, concluded. Words used to hold up my world, to construct it, to protect me from it. Now they are transparent and suddenly fragile. Now, they offer me no comfort at all. Now, they say: *giving comfort is not what we do. Not anymore. Now we do something else.*

And I ask: *what?*

And they say: *find out.*

10.

It's a Sunday in April and I am at home. I have a whole day to spend outside. We have herbs to plant, and onion sets, and heather. We have beds to dig and grass to cut. Spring is roaring out. Time is pressing.

My nine-year-old daughter, Leela, appears by my side. 'Hello, Daddy,' she says. 'Would you like to come to my stone-carving workshop?'

'Er,' I say. 'Yes, that would be great.' She leads me to an upturned box in the porch on which lie a selection of scratched stones she has found in the garden. She hands me an awl and a lump of sandstone.

'How long will it take?' I ask.

'About 20 minutes,' she says.

'I've only got 10,' I say, instinctively.

'Oh, that's OK,' she says. 'You can still do something good. You have to decide what you want to carve. Maybe a lady's face, or maybe Quincy.'

Quincy is our dog. I sit on a stool and begin to carve the dog's face on the stone. *Shit*, I think to myself, for the eight-hundredth time. *I am a terrible father.* The thing that has haunted me throughout my children's lives has been the remembered moments. We all have them: standout images from our childhood, times, pictures, events, things which sank in, good or bad. But there's no rhyme or reason to them. You never know what they will take with them into adulthood. Will Leela always remember the time we camped together in the woods by Lough Gill, just yards from Yeats' Isle of Innisfree, and cooked dinner over a fire? Will she remember us playing vets together in a garden beneath a volcano in Chilean Patagonia? Will she remember us sheltering from the rain in a Cumbrian wood? Or will she remember the time I couldn't spare 10 minutes because I had to do something which I had told myself was more important than being with her, because it was 'work,' and 'work' is always more important than living?

Part of my plan, when we came here, was that my newfound rootedness would spread like a slow mist into every other area of my life. My restless energy would be channeled into planting trees, clearing brambles, building treehouses, hacking down long grass, hefting stones and all the other heavy, ongoing work of running a working smallholding. The time I spend in my head, writing and thinking, which in the past had nearly eaten me alive so often, would be balanced by time outside, in the sun and rain, using my hands instead of my brain. I would tame my monkey mind, force myself out from my internal world into the external one, at least for a little while, and this would save me and those around me.

This wasn't such a bad plan, and it has worked to a degree. There is nothing like setting a rat trap or carrying a bucket full of shit in the rain to force you back into the real stuff of life. But if you have that monkey mind, as I suppose all writers—all humans?—do, this stuff is not going to keep you occupied for very long. The dark truth, which any writer or artist, or indeed reader or music-lover, will know is that the worlds we create inside us are often simply better than the one we are forced to live in. I don't want this to be true, but it is. I still enjoy carrying buckets of shit in the rain, and I enjoy catching rats too. Everyone's inner sadist needs a regular, healthy outing. But being here has not calmed me as I hoped it would. It has not saved me and it is not going to, and I have taken too long to understand that.

Here we are, staring into the timeless gulf between ideal and reality. I have come to hate idealists like the one I used to be, as a born-again non-smoker hates the smell of tobacco. Ideals are a pox on humanity: if you have ideals, you will go out into the world as a destroyer. You will always see what doesn't work rather than what does, you will always be able to leap into the space between things as they are and things as, in your narrow view, they should be. Then you will try to close the space, to heal it, and you will end up either clinically depressed or running a series of death camps, or—the worst possible outcome—both. As any Buddhist master will tell you, repeatedly for several lifetimes, the only way to free yourself from this trap is simply to *be*. To pay attention. *It is what it is*, they will say, patiently, as your Western, university-trained mind screams, *what it is isn't good enough! Make it better!*

I talked to Jyoti about this. I said: I wanted to be one of these dads who plays with their kids all day, who crawls about on all fours with them riding on his back, who is genial and avuncular and never impatient. I was going to be rooted and stolid and reliable, like an old tree. But I can't turn my head off. And she said: you were never going to be that kind of dad, if they even exist, so why don't you stop trying to be one? They love you for who you are. They can see that you live in your head, because everybody can. They know you're like Uncle Quentin out of The *Famous Five*. Why did you think that was going to change?

I thought the land was going to change me, I mumbled.

Oh, honestly, she said.

I thought I'd get here and reach a plateau, I said. I thought the journey would be over then, and I could concentrate on just being. Digging in, honing my skills, becoming calmer, wiser, steadier. I thought I'd arrived. But maybe it's not a plateau after all. Maybe there aren't ever any plateaus.

The plateau, she said, comes when you're dead.

11.

I wanted to be a tree, but I am not a tree. I wanted to sing to the forest, but no one ever taught me the words, and I don't suppose they ever will because there is no one in my world to teach me. Nobody here has known the words for centuries. I was born in those rootless suburbs and they have given me a rootless soul. I am not a tree. I am some kind of slinking animal in the hedge-row. I am a seed on the wind. I am water. I am coming to the rocks at the lip of the fall.

12.

I was writing a book. I usually am. Last winter, I started writing it. It worked for a while, and then it ground to a halt. This is common enough. Books stop and start, they go through rough patches and charmed patches. But this time, something different was happening. I could feel it. There was something missing; some energy. It wasn't 'writer's block,' because I could still write—here I am, still writing. So what was it? What was happening here?

I realized, after a while, that anything I have ever written in the past which has even approached being any good at all has been written from some place of desperation. It has been written from the edges: from the dark slope of the mountain, not the warmth of the campfire. I have been writing in, not writing out. I have been shouting something, in the expectation that I would never be heard. Now I had to face—I still have to face—a possibility I don't know what to do with. Maybe I can't write anything from the campfire. Here, in this settled place, in this comfortable place. Maybe I need to be desperate again. Maybe I need to be bare and hungry on the mountain. But what does that mean? What would it look like? Where did the words go, and what do they want? I don't seem to be able to write anything but questions anymore. See?

Out in the field now, among the poppies and the cornflowers, among the creeping buttercup and the walnut trees smothered by couch grass, under the elders and the daytime moon, something is whispering to me what the headless statue once whispered to Rilke: *you must change your life.*

Oh, God, I think. *Not again.*

13.

When did magic disappear? When did stones stop talking? When did birds stop relaying messages to me, and tree spirits stop replying when I left gifts for them in the knots of their trunks which twisted around and reached upward at the same time? That's what children have that adults don't. That's the Garden we can never get back to. Maybe that's the glimpse we have of the kind of mind that sings those songs to the forest. Sometimes Leela sings to the field or the trees, though she likes to do it in private. She does it less now than she used to. She is on the cusp of losing it. I don't want her to know it.

The cultures of the Papuan Highlands developed in isolation for tens of thousands of years until the 20th century, when airplanes and empires began the unraveling. The Papuans have suffered decades of colonization, convincing claims of attempted genocide, aggressive Christian evangelism, the pollution, abuse, and theft of their land and all of the other horrors that settled civilizations always inflict on tribal people when they find them, as if they were ashamed of what they had become and wanted to wipe out the evidence that it was still possible to be something else. Patricide, matricide, slaughter of the ancestors. But the Papuans still sing to the forest. We grow out of that when we're about 10. What are we missing that they can still see? What took the songs away?

Leela and her six-year-old brother Jeevan have an area of our land they call Wildy. It's a strip of undergrowth, trees, and chaotic unkempt hedgerow that separates our lane from the neighboring field and they live in it, sometimes, when the fancy takes them. Wildy is strewn with old upturned wooden chairs and plastic tubs and bent pans they have been using in some domestic drama. Adults are barred from Wildy; it's a place where children talk to fairies and birds and trees and the spirits that inhabit them.

When I first got here I strained myself to rediscover the lost magic, to see if I could hear the songs. I thought that maybe— just maybe—if I paid enough attention I could enter the Garden again. It was always a longshot, but I had to try. I listened to the birds a lot—our land is ripe with birdsong—and I watched them. I tried to watch them without naming them, though it went against my intellectual, analytical instincts. I didn't always succeed, because I can't resist the impulse to catalog. I've been making a list for three years of all the birds that visit our land in the course of the year. Wagtail. Bullfinch. Dunnock. Wren. Collared dove. Robin. Long-tailed tit. Goldfinch. Swift. Swallow. Blackcap. Coal tit. Willow warbler. Sparrowhawk. Fieldfare. Pheasant. Heron. These are the edited highlights.

It's spring as I write this. A few months back, in February, I got up early most days and walked from the house to my writing cabin in the field before anyone else was up and while it was still dark. Often, as first light appeared, there would be a fat yellow-bellied song thrush on the very top branch of the old elder tree near the cabin, and he would sing, in repeating patterns, the same tune twice, then another, then another. I would stand on the porch and listen and tell myself to give him the correct quality of attention. My kids would just have heard him, reacted, moved on, but I stood there listening rapt while, at the same time, berating myself for not having the kind of spontaneous experience of the thrush's song that I wanted to have and I felt I ought to be able to have, especially if I was going to write books with thrushes' songs in them.

The Earth, says the French philosopher Gaston Bachelard, wants to be *admired* by us. Rilke agrees: 'Everything beckons us to perceive it,' he tells us, 'whispers at every turn, *Remember me.*' Does the thrush want me to perceive it, to admire it? Does the world want to be remembered? Don't we all? Why else would anybody write a book?

14.

The land is warming with the approach of summer, and the budding season has begun. The green fire is flashing out from the tree tips, the broccoli is flowering, the grasses are heaving themselves into life again. The air above the field is criss-crossed with traffic patterns of rooks heading for the spruce trees with beaks full of dry couch and whitethorn. It's time to sit down by the fire with our basket of seeds and plan what to plant this year and where. It's time to talk about getting hens and how to keep the foxes away from them and how to build a rabbit fence and what varieties of potatoes to get to avoid the blight that killed most of the crop last year.

But instead I have to go away. Because I am not a real farmer I have to make my money in other places. I need the Internet or the Dublin-to-Holyhead ferry and sometimes both to put food on my family's table. I can only live here without being here sometimes, and although I want to change that I also don't want to change that. I want to write, not drive tractors to and from the slurry tank. Still, when spring calls me away just as life is roaring out I get resentful. This is the time of year when, more than any other, I find I can sometimes actually be here; can sometimes feel I am close to belonging. I don't want to leave, which has to be a good sign.

I don't want to leave, but I have to. When I feel like this, I remind myself that I could instead be sitting at a desk in an office every day doing a job I hate to pay a mortgage on a house I don't like in a town I never wanted to live in, and that instead I live on a piece of beautiful land and write books for a living and get to teach interesting people sometimes and so I should shut up and check my privilege.

This time around I am teaching a course at a college in Devon. It's a course I helped to design, about making art in times of crisis. I don't really want to be here. The people are interesting, the college does good work, two or three years ago I would have been enthused, but something is happening to me or is continuing to happen, the thing that began when I arrived here or was brought into focus by that arrival. Everything is being upended inside me and I don't know what is happening or why. A chapter in my life is ending and I have been putting off that reality for too long, holding it at arm's length. But being here, doing this, a thing which I have outlived now, has made it clear that I must run home and jump. Into what? I don't know. But you never have a choice when the wheel turns like this. You jump, or you will be pushed over the side.

There's a little outdoor classroom in the woods here. It's a lovely space, some curved wooden benches surrounded by Scots pines and oaks. My teaching colleague and I sit on two small benches in front of 24 assembled students, who look at us expectantly with their notebooks open. The birds sing, clouds pass above the blue, the air breathes us in. My colleague is talking at length about something or other and I listen to his words flow out of his mouth up into the trees and dissolve in irrelevance. The trees don't care. The birds aren't listening. The students are listening, the humans are paying attention, to us the words are connections, they have meaning, but I see suddenly that his words and mine, all the words, are just crackling into the light of the day, spreading like ash, rising like smoke invisible. The concepts, the air.

None of this is real. The Scots pine is real, it is a being, a presence, the birds are real, the solidity of the Earth is real and the words are nothing. Nothing. The words are not alive. The words are not quickened, they do not dance or stagger, they are not inhabited. They are hammered survey stakes, acrylic falsehoods that die in the reality of the place. All humans do is talk. Talk talk talk and out come the sounds and like poetry they change nothing but we talk talk talk anyway and we mistake the sounds for meaning or action, and the trees stand there silently and we just talk. My words do not dance because there is no magic in them, and unless there is magic in them nobody should speak words. How would we live if the only words we spoke were as solid as this great giant of a tree that has been standing here for a century? Has there been a culture, a people, for whom that was true?

What if I just shut up?

In the evening, I go to a talk put on at the college by a mythologist from Botswana named Colin Campbell. He grew up amongst the San people and, despite being white, has been a *sangoma*, a traditional healer, from a young age. He is grey-haired and slight and softly spoken but can hold the silent attention of 50 people for half an hour by telling a story which, in our terms, doesn't necessarily even make sense. Take a story from a place and drop it into another place and it doesn't necessarily make sense, at least not at first. Like people, stories don't always travel well. Nothing belongs everywhere, and some things only belong somewhere. But some stories, when they travel, can spark strange new things in unmeasured hearts.

Colin talks about fire and water, the two elements, the two archetypal forces within us. They turn and dance around each other hourly and daily and their dance makes our life. Fire seeks to evaporate water, water seeks to put out fire, neither triumphs and the dance goes on. Fire is the upward force. It roars out, overcomes, climbs, triumphs, pushes above and beyond. Water is the downward force. It drags you back to places, wants to belong, holds you, spreads you out, tugs you within. In traditional Botswana, says Campbell, men are fire and women are water. When a girl begins to menstruate she is taken down to the river for her initiation, which is in the water. A woman's blood connects her with, draws her back into, the Earth. The women gather in the river to initiate the girl into the tribe, to bring her into her womanhood, to mingle her body's blood with the water that flows down to the sea.

If a woman's water draws her back to the Earth, a man's fire tears him away from it. Women are born attached to the Earth, but men are born apart from it, and this makes men more dangerous. A man's initiation, his rite of passage from boyhood to manhood, is external. The men disappear for months or even years into the mountains or the bush, and there they encounter death. Some will not come back from the journey, but those who do will have been drawn into the adult world by this meeting with death. They are taken away to learn to come back again, and when they come back, and the women come back, fire meets water and the dance begins.

If the sexes are divided by the elements, says Campbell, so are the two halves of our lives, all of us, men and women. The first half of our lives is fire, the second water. In our young lives we rage away from the Earth, from each other, from our families and our given roles, from strictures, rules, and places. We are pulled by ambition, desire, excitement, greed, the seeking of newness, the need to break away. The second half of our lives is water: it is a dropping back towards Earth, a making of families, a sometimes painful understanding of self, a rooting in place, a coming home. The transition between the two phases, from young to old, youth to midlife, is a process of cooling fire, of moving into water time. Where Campbell comes from, this means that the soul, or the pysche, or the true self, is calling us home. Sometimes we resist the call, hold on tightly to the fire, believe that without the fire we are dead. In fact, without the fire we are just beginning to live again, only as something subtly new.

Sitting now in this little wood-paneled room, listening to the softly spoken man, I recognize myself. I recognize my turn away, my retreat to my new place, the simplicities I was seeking and maybe why the simplicities are not enough either. Nothing is ever enough if you go out there looking. Hearing this, I understand why I often wake up in the morning now wondering why I bother to do anything at all. I understand why these days I can't write, or increasingly even talk, about politics, why I shy away from expressing strong opinions in a way that would once have seemed unfathomable to me. I understand why I am sometimes overcome by an unruly desire to be a hermit or a monk, why I sabotage myself the minute I begin to do anything that feels like ambition. I'm being pulled down into the water. It is not my fire time. Not anymore.

As he finishes talking, Campbell wonders whether humanity might be experiencing a midlife crisis. We have been fire, we have built and controlled and expanded and triumphed. Now we look around at our triumph and suddenly we feel we can't understand the meaning of any of it. What was it for? What was the point? We look at the changing climate and the fallen trees and the plastic in the oceans and the anomie of our phone-drugged children and something tells us we are disconnected but we don't know what to do with this feeling. We need to move, are called to move, from fire to water, but there is nobody holding this ritual for us, nobody to organize our trip to the river or the mountain. And so we stumble on alone, and our smartphone apps and robots that can order a curry for us from the Internet and toy drones for Christmas and regular doses of antidepressants and celebrity TV—all the great swirling ocean of bullshit we have surrounded ourselves with in lieu of life, in lieu of *living*—this is our civilization's equivalent of a middle-aged executive buying a red sports car and sleeping with his secretary.

But you get through a midlife crisis, don't you? Or you should. You could. If you handle it well, you mature and you learn. You move from fire into water. You let go and the water pulls you down over the falls and you end up nowhere near either where you started or where you thought you would go. The fall is as inevitable for us as it is for rain. By clinging to fire, we get burnt. By falling into water, we float.

Or, we drown.

Where Campbell grew up in Southern Africa, when the adolescent boys went out for their rite of passage into the wild places, they either came back a man or they didn't come back at all. Perhaps we are all together now, heading for the bush. Perhaps it is time. But I only want to bow my head and be silent. I only want, now, to be swimming away.

15

This business of silence: it has been crawling towards me for years, like an injured man begging for help. I said earlier that I felt called. I often feel called now. Sometimes I think I am being called by God, and that seems embarrassing to write down, and self-regarding. Still, others have felt the same. R. S. Thomas wrote of the function of silence in searching for what he called, in his poem of the same name, 'The Presence':

> *It has the universe*
>> *to be abroad in.*
> *There is nothing I can do*
> *but fill myself with my own*
>> *silence, hoping it will approach*
>> *like a wild creature to drink*
> *there, or perhaps like Narcissus*
> *to linger a moment over its transparent face.*

If it's not God, perhaps it is my true self I can hear, whatever that means. Perhaps it is the water in me. Perhaps it is my psyche or my soul. Perhaps part of my unconscious mind is telling part of my conscious mind, for its own good, what it needs to do to survive, which right now is to shut up. To pay attention. To reconsider. I don't know. I'm not a theologian or a physician or a psychiatrist. I'm a writer, which means that I aim myself at all of those things but fall short at all of them most of the time. Writers fall short at everything except creating sentences. This is what we really like to do: put words in an order which can conjure something real but unseen in the air around us, and around you when you read what we have put down. Really, this business of sentences is the only thing we can do and the only thing that motivates us. All the rest—the stories, the characters, the metaphors, the morals and the messages—they come later, with varying degrees of success. Everything is built on the sentences. We just love sentences, and we can't get proper jobs.

The silence: it has been crawling at me, and I have been walking fast from it, afraid. I grew up thinking that words, sentences, metaphors, were what I did, that my work was to get better at them until I could blow away the world and myself, and get the girls in the process. But for years they have been surrounded by this creeping silence, which has soaked towards them like an ink spill and threatened their very definition. Every time I turn around there it is, a little closer now.

The silence tells me that the words are a problem. That the talking is a problem. That what I need is stillness. It was the silence that took me from England to Ireland, from the town to the country. It was the silence that made me close down my social media accounts, withdraw more and more from the Internet, stop reading the news or writing about it. It was the silence that pulled me away, inward, pulled me down like the rain into the ocean. I didn't know what was going on at all. And now the silence, sometimes, tells me that the journey will not be complete until these words are silent too. That's the bit that frightens me. That's the bit I hold off with verve and fear. The silence says: *now is not the time for words.* The silence says: *pay attention.*

Can you write from silence? Could I write a silent book, consisting of nothing but blank pages? John Cage did something similar with music. Some people thought he was ludicrous, others profound, but Cage knew that silence itself was a quality, not simply a gap between noises. He first realized this on entering a soundproof booth in a recording studio and discovering that it was not, as he had expected, devoid of sounds. 'I heard two sounds, one high and one low,' he recounted. 'When I described them to the engineer in charge, he informed me that the high one was my nervous system in operation, the low one my blood in circulation.' Silence had its own soundscape. It was not an absence of something; rather, it was a different quality of something. It had a personality. It *was*.

Where I live, I can hear the wind, the birdsong, sometimes a tractor, often the rain; and I can hear the silence, in between and around and creeping through all of these things. In the city I heard cars and people, sometimes airplanes. I heard the twittering and chirping of civilization. But no silence, not even in the deepest hour of the night. We are building a world in which silence is a crime: a waste of something. An empty thing which must be filled. Ours is a world of metaphors and sentences, unpunctuated, flowing on faster and faster, building in rhythm and urgency until they crash, fatally, into the last page of the book.

I don't know what this is. But even when I try to write myself away from it, it comes back around. It is after me. It has nearly caught me. Do you see?

16.

I feel like I am being broken open by something, cracked like a nut, split in the sun and left to dry. I feel like there is a hole in the sky through which the words have always poured down into me, and that if the correct ceremonies are not directed to the correct gods the hole will close up and that will be the end. I feel like that would be the end of me. I feel like writing is an act of service, or should be, and that you must decide who or what you are going to serve. I feel like that decision is sometimes taken out of your hands. I feel that is happening to me right now.

I feel like a person is a process, not a thing. I feel like the hole in the sky shifts with the cloud banks and the winds, and that you have to follow it. I feel that there is no plateau, ever. I feel that it is good to spend some time by the campfire, that we all need it, that I need it, but that I have to retreat back up the mountain after a while. I feel like I can't take too much warmth. I feel like I have no choice at all in any of this.

I feel that words are savage gods and that in the end, however well you serve them, they will eat you alive.

17.

A commissioning editor writes to me. She has heard that I have a new book coming out. Would I like to write an opinion piece for her newspaper to promote it? I tell her that I try not to have opinions anymore. She explains that the opinions don't have to be political. In fact, they have too many of those. Everyone has political opinions. I could write about something else if I liked—something domestic, for example, or artistic. Anything, really, as long as it has 'a strong line of argument.'

A strong line of argument. Ten years ago, even five, I'd have leapt at the offer. I could argue about anything, everything, and I did. I was that kind of writer, that kind of person, for a long while, for too long. I thought the world could be patterned and marked and laid out labeled on a table. I thought I could argue my way around the gap between the ideal and the reality.

I thought I could make it all fit if I could just muster enough cleverness.

But the world is not short of cleverness and not much is right. Now I know this is a god my words refuse to serve. No more cleverness. No more opinions. Opinions are easy to come by. Stillness is the really hard work. Not knowing is the hardest work of all. Even writing those two words fills me with anxiety. *Not knowing.* Not knowing. Not knowing anything at all. But that's where we all find ourselves, most of the time. We just won't admit it.

'Can we remain unmoving?' asks Zen teacher Charlotte Joko Beck. 'Can we keep our mouths shut until the right action or the right word arises by itself? Most of the time, there's no harm in doing *nothing*. Most of what we do doesn't make much difference, anyway; we just think it does.'

Can I keep my mouth shut? I've never even asked that question before.

Now: is this why the silence is coming for me? Because my writing, for so long, has been a struggle, a battle to the death between a poet and an evangelist, and that I will the poet onwards, but the evangelist has too often come out on top? Perhaps the evangelist can be smothered with the silence. Or perhaps that's idiotic: perhaps fire needs water, perhaps poet and evangelist must work together or else there would be too much fire or too much water in these words.

I don't know about that, but I know about this: I can't write about politics or ideas anymore. I can't write in theories, I can't draw out grand concepts until they are stretched so painfully thin that they snap. I can't tell you how to live. Not a line of it, not a word.

> *Free thinker! Do you think you are the only thinker*
> *on this earth in which life blazes inside all things?*
> *Your liberty does what it wishes with the powers it controls,*
> *but when you gather to plan, the universe is not there.*[1]

Once I had a thousand feelings and I tried to pretend they were thoughts. Now I have somewhere to belong to but I still feel lost, and I don't know what that means. Can words, can writing, bore a hole through this dimness? Sometimes, more often each day, they seem like a veiling, not a revelation.

18.

What is writing? It is the basis of civilization, or one of them. The others are agriculture, cities, war, and government. Once you have agriculture, you need to count—to keep a tally of how much grain you've grown, how many cattle are in your herd, how much tax you have to pay to the newly powerful rulers growing fat on your surplus and building armies with the resulting income. The first written accounts are just that—accounts, on clay tablets. But this kind of writing, the kind I am doing now, this baring, this strange persuasion: what is it? This kind of stuff is not a direct reporting of external realities, it is the representation of internal experience. But what is it for? Why write it down? Am I trying to direct your thoughts here, or mine? I have been doing this all of my adult life, and I have never asked this question. It has seemed enough to *feel* something

---

1   "Golden Lines," Gérard de Nerval, translated by Robert Bly

strongly and then rush to get it on paper. Some passion will descend, sometimes at the most awkward moments, some sentence will make itself known, something will become clear, and if at that moment you don't have a notebook you are doomed. I don't usually have a notebook. I find myself squatting on station platforms, scribbling on the back of receipts. I find myself at parties, running to an upstairs bedroom and rifling through strangers' drawers for a pen. I find myself in a green wood in summer, sifting through my raincoat for any scrap, any stub. I am woefully unprepared, always, for what comes.

Now I ask myself why I do this and I don't know what the answer is. I have never had, before now, to even ask. I had never thought I would. And here's my fear, I think, here's what is perhaps at the root of my loss of confidence in these black symbols on white paper: I worry that all words are lies. That all abstractions are figments, and argumentative words, the construction of positions, the worst lies of all. Maybe the form builds the shape of the lies. Californian poet Robinson Jeffers explained why he only wrote poetry by saying, 'I can tell lies in prose.' What if all prose is a lie? What if all words are as fake as a scratch on a clay tablet denoting a cow? It is not a cow. It is a scratch. It will never be anything other than a scratch. To see the real cow, you have to go outside.

19.

The cultural ecologist David Abram, in his book *The Spell of the Sensuous*, claims to have identified the moment when written language jumped the boundary from rootedness to abstraction. The building blocks of Semitic written language—the *aleph-beth*—he explains, were a series of characters each based on a consonant in spoken language. There were 22 of them, and with their advent 'a new distance opens between human culture and the rest of nature.' Why? Because, unlike every written language before it (Egyptian hieroglyphics perhaps being the best-known example) the *aleph-beth*—which later became, via the Greeks, our own *alphabet*—was made up of written characters which no longer directly represented an actual thing out in the real world.

The original letter *A*, writes Abram, may once have represented the shape of an ox's head; *O* may have been an eye; *Q* the back end and tail of a monkey. But once the Semites got hold of them, turned them into abstract symbols and wrote them down—with the Greeks later finishing the job—the link between culture and nature was finally lost. Written language was no longer visually tied to the world of physical, real, naturally occurring things. Letters were now only marks, signifying nothing but their own internal meaning.

These gestures on parchment could not be used to sing to a forest, only to speak to other people. Human language now pointed to nothing but itself. It was a code which only other humans could interpret, and it formed an auditory loop, like a guitar held too close to an amp, forever issuing screeching feedback into our minds.

20.

'In the middle of the journey of our life,' writes Dante, in the very first lines of *Inferno*, 'I found myself in a dark wood, where the straight path had been lost.'

I think I have walked into some wood, and lost sight of my words in the dimness. I thought I knew what words were for and how to use them. But I thought I knew a lot of things and suddenly, now, in the last year perhaps, none of them seem to matter at all. Where did my strong political views go? I used to know how the world ought to work. I used to know what I wanted to say, to think, to write. Now I don't know why I would ever have thought that. I used to know that living on a smallholding with my family would be the end of a journey, a contentment. I used to think, or pretend to think, that a racing, restless soul could be stilled by grass and trees and the daily work of being. But whatever pushes my words out into the world is not still or calm. That small animal never sleeps and it never will. And I am tired from wrestling with it for so long. I am so tired now.

When I reached the plateau, there was no view of the landscape around and beneath. Instead there was this dark wood. There was no wood on the map I was carrying.

A reader once emailed me about my novel *The Wake*, in which pagan gods and broken Anglo-Saxon warriors converse for 300 pages in a language I made up for the occasion. The email was so good that I kept it. *oh my fucking god paul kingsnorth*, it began, promisingly and all in lower case. *the wake is quite the deepest darkest wood to wander in. so disorientating. writing it must have led you to some strange strange places indeed. i can barely imagine spending the day wrangling that beast and then going down to make dinner for the kids.*

I didn't really think about the implications at the time because I was too busy feeling flattered, and I had to make dinner for the kids. But then a friend said something similar to me a while later. 'How can you write like that, and then just come back to your family and try and act normal?' she asked. Write like what?

I wondered. What do you mean *act normal*? It was just what I did. It didn't occur to me that it was a balancing act. Could it be I didn't realize the price I would have to pay down the line for 'writing like that'? Could it be that wrangling the beast leads you towards exhaustion, even injury? Could it be that the well is deep but not inexhaustible? Could it be that the beast and the children, the words and the peaceful landscape I wanted to draw them from, are a threat to each other? That the gods don't mix?

21.

'Great novels,' writes Milan Kundera, 'are always a little more intelligent than their authors.'

22.

Words, for me, have always been everything. They overlay everything I see and walk through, like a set of grid lines which make sense of and measure a landscape. They are my means of understanding the scale of what I am looking at. My mind responds not to images, sounds, even emotions, but to words. I listen to music and it's the lyrics that speak to me. I read the lyric sheets inside the CD boxes while the tune plays. When I see a piece of art I look around for the explanatory leaflet. I feel an emotion and I want it explained in words, I want it analyzed, laid out for me, because it's easier than feeling it properly and it makes more sense. I read a poem, and nobody needs to explain it. I write a book and everything is explained.

Words are my gateway. They always have been, I think, since I was a child. They take me into, through, beyond, the reality I share with other people. And sometimes, words make you promises. *No matter how much you fuck up*, say the words, *we will be there to save you. Whatever happens, you can write your way through it. We are your lifebelt, your raft, your parachute. We will always save you from your own consequence.*

Without my words, there is no path at all through this wood.

But now something is wrong with my words.

Something has happened, and I don't know what it is. I could cling to words, once, use them to explain myself, bend them to my will, enslave them. But now there is some flaw in them, some resistance. Within them, something stumbles. The animal that makes them is sick, or in refusal. The gods won't play. I have words, still—look, here they are. But it feels as if they are playing with me. I set them to run in some direction and they veer off course, jump the fences, make joyfully for the ocean. They have broken their chains, at last. *Not this time!* they laugh as they run. *We're in charge now!*

Do I sit down here, in this small clearing in the light, or do I stumble on into the undergrowth? How do I know which is the right direction?

23.

Here is Russell Means, member of the Oglala Lakota people, of the Sioux Tribe, activist in the American Indian Movement, occupier of Alcatraz and Wounded Knee. Means has riled people on his side and others with his work. Politics has got him into trouble, and he doesn't even like politics. In fact, he hates it; it is a means to an end, for him, but the end is deeper than anything that can be expressed in political language. And he hates talking about it, or at least writing about it, because he hates writing too. In 1980, Means agrees to give a speech about what he stands for, but only on the basis that he doesn't have to write it down. He starts it like this:

> *The only possible opening for a statement of this kind is that I detest writing. The process itself epitomizes the European concept of 'legitimate' thinking; what is written has an importance that is denied the spoken. My culture, the Lakota culture, has an oral tradition, so I ordinarily reject writing. It is one of the white world's ways of destroying the cultures of non-European peoples, the imposing of an abstraction over the spoken relationship of a people.*

He's got the crowd's attention now, and he goes on to give a long and powerful speech about the need for American Indians to resist Europeanization. This is not just a matter of fighting for political rights, he says. There is a whole worldview involved, and it is deeper, wider and more disturbing than most people, including most American Indians, in his view, will give credit for. It's not a question of Marxism versus capitalism, religion versus secularism, right versus left. These, according to Means, are just different shards of the same broken window:

> *Newton, for example, 'revolutionized' physics and the so-called natural sciences by reducing the physical universe to a linear mathematical equation. Descartes did the same thing with culture. John Locke did it with politics, and Adam Smith did it with economics. Each one of these 'thinkers' took a piece of the spirituality of human existence and converted it into a code, an abstraction ... Each*

of these intellectual revolutions served to abstract the
European mentality even further, to remove the wonderful
complexity and spirituality from the universe and replace
it with a logical sequence: one, two, three. Answer!

Unlike me, it seems, Means does not have a European mind, and
no European expectations rest on his shoulders and so he is not
scared of the call or the silence. He is not afraid to use a word
like 'spirituality' in public. He knows why people sing to the forest. Maybe he sings himself.

Where is my European mind leading me? Where do these
abstractions end?

The European materialist tradition of despiritualizing the
universe is very similar to the mental process which goes
into dehumanizing another person ... In terms of the despir-
itualization of the universe, the mental process works so
that it becomes virtuous to destroy the planet. Terms like
progress and development are used as cover words here,
the way victory and freedom are used to justify butchery
in the dehumanization process. For example, a real-estate
speculator may refer to 'developing' a parcel of ground by
opening a gravel quarry; development here means total,
permanent destruction, with the earth itself removed. But
European logic has gained a few tons of gravel with which
more land can be 'developed' through the construction of
road beds. Ultimately, the whole universe is open—in the
European view—to this sort of insanity.

Sometimes—not often enough—when I have squatted around
mountain fires or sat in straw-laid houses in jungle valleys, and
I have listened to those tribal people speak, usually through trans-
lators, I have felt at home. Not because of the way they lived, or
because of their cultural particularities—what they wore, what

they ate, how they worked and organized themselves—some of which my European mind felt alienated from or was even offended by. No, I felt at home because they said, almost casually, the kind of thing that Russell Means is saying here more angrily. *Well of course*, they would say, *the Earth is alive. Of course everything is sacred. Why would you think otherwise?*

When I hear or read this, straight from the heart of a much older culture, I am always, no matter how many times it happens, brought up short. In moments like that I, someone who, in common with those of my class, nation, and generation, has never really belonged anywhere, feel curiously *at home*. Is this what I have been looking for all along? Some old home I never had? These people I have somehow felt connected to, though they are so distant from me in almost every way: they know how to be part of a world that is alive, and that, for them, is a very practical proposition.

I have always felt the world was alive and speaking, ever since I was a child, and I have always wanted to sit around that campfire, even if just for a moment, like my children can still sit in Wildy and talk to the birds. And when I do sit around those fires, so very rarely, I understand, maybe, who I am, or once was, and what I am trying to get back to and why it takes me so many words to say it and why I so often get it wrong. I am using the wrong language. I am in the wrong world. Nobody knows how to hear, and I don't know how to speak.

If I wanted to live that way, where would I go? What would I do? Russell Means may despise what he calls the 'European mind' but he makes clear, later in his speech, that it's the mind he takes issue with, not the body. Native Americans can have European minds too, he says. As for Europeans—any of them who resist this desacralizing of the world, this colonizing, this building and profiteering, this digging and burning—as far as he's concerned, they stand on the side of virtue. We can argue over the way he uses the word 'European' if we want to—and I probably would—but we can all see what he's saying if we're not wilfully blind, and it's something I've believed in—no, it's something I've *felt*—for as long as I can remember. *Of course the Earth is alive. Of course.*

Somebody once told me, commenting on an article I'd written about something or other, that I was a 'pre-modern thinker.' It wasn't an insult, just an observation, and it brought me up short because I saw that it was true, and also terrible. I realized that all this scrabbling towards 'belonging' somewhere, towards rooting myself in something, all this puzzlement over how and what to be—it was some clutching towards a notion of being *indigenous.* That was what I wanted: to live in a culture which thinks the world is a sacred thing, for which reality is, as it was for the Lakota, a flaming hoop, whose language is the language of beauty and fire, which sings to the forest and expects it to hear. I have always wanted to be part of a culture which walks through the wild world as if it were *of* it, which doesn't talk of carbon or biodiversity or profit or growth but talks and lives as if this way of speaking were the poisonous bullshit that it so obviously is.

That's what I have wanted. That would be a living world. That is the world that humans lived in for 99 percent of our history. Why would we imagine it was not still swimming in our veins? Maybe it is, and maybe we know it. Maybe people like me were forged in the breaking of that world. Maybe our European minds grew like weeds from the rubble of the old cultures which managed to live well in the world for 200,000 years without fucking the whole place up. Maybe we are an invasive species, we who think the world is a Machine we can take apart and examine. Us, with our letters, our concepts, our plans. Us, with our writing.

Was this indigeneity, this burning hoop, this old world, what I was looking for when I came here, even if I didn't know it? A world without writing, a world before abstract symbols? Echoes of it, at least? It's ridiculous, surely. And yet sometimes I think I do hear echoes, in the field in the still of night, and they bounce off me like bat sonar from the walls of a cave because I do not live in a culture like that. I live in this one, and I cannot escape it because it is all around me and it is in me and I will carry it, like a dormant virus, as long as I live.

I walk the world looking for something to belong to, but there is nothing to belong to because there is no culture for us anymore, only civilization, and they are not the same thing. There is no connection between the wild and the tame, the human and the beyond-human, the sacred and the profane. In the world I was born in, Eros and Psyche have gone their separate ways, and now my words are eating themselves alive.

24.

A few nights ago, I was at a birthday party on a friend's farm. There was a bonfire, and the kids were playing around it. A cake had just arrived, with candles. The day had been warm but the night was coming down now, a spare crescent hung in the sky and the cold was sharp in my nostrils.

I went for a piss in a hedge. I turned back, buttoning myself up, and looked down the slope to the fire. Half-lit figures laughed and drank. I turned again: through the window of a mobile home, a lampshade, starlit in orange. A wooden outbuilding, two polytunnels. In the encroaching dark, the air blue, the horizon smoky orange, it all looked like a painting.

And it always looks like a painting, everything, to me. The world happens on the other side of a thin gauze and I can only ever break through by accident and all my life the gauze has been there and I have never believed in the world, have never believed it was real, and the only time I have ever really, truly felt alive, ever really felt I could break through it, tear it, come out into the real

has been when I am writing.

I'm writing this now alone in my freezing car at the farm's edge, by a rushing river, with a pen I found in the door and a scrap of paper from the dashboard. I can't feel my toes. The world pumps like blood when I make these marks; at other times, the blood pools, tepid and waiting. And still I never remember to bring a notebook.

25.

Most Wednesday nights I cycle down to the local pub to meet my friend Mark. The pub is a small one-room affair in a rural hamlet with a dartboard, a pool table, a TV, a peat fire, and five or six men lined up at the bar with pints of stout. We add to their number weekly for two or three pints of Guinness, a game of chess or darts, both usually lost by me, and some conversation about the state of the world. Mark and I both like conversations about the state of the world, and we both come at it from the same kind of direction, only he is more committed to the business of escape than me. He once lived for two years in a caravan without handling money, and he now lives in a self-built off-grid cabin with no running water or electricity. Last year he chucked out his phone and his laptop. If you want to contact him now you have to drop by or write a letter. It's quite a nice discipline, though awkward if you need to cancel your pub date on a Wednesday morning.

In his heart, and sometimes in his head, Mark is a primitivist. He's convinced that the default state for human beings is hunting and gathering in small bands in a wild world, and that most of what has happened since the development of agriculture has been a spiraling down towards doom. Mark, like me, has a sense that something fundamental has been disconnected in our circuitry, and that this is demonstrated when people like me write sentences about human beings which use the word 'circuitry' to describe their inner workings, as if they were bloody machines, which they may be soon but are not yet. For a while he toyed with the idea that his primitivism could be a political project: that somehow we could work towards a resetting of humanity, that we could crash the system and go back to the Garden. This is a mistake we all make. These days he is more philosophical, and concentrates his energies on learning to fish and butcher deer, neither of which he is yet anything like good enough at to survive an apocalypse.

As both a primitivist and a writer—a combination which is itself a farcical contradiction, as we both know—Mark understands my collapse of confidence in the written word, and like me he sometimes asks himself if, after a while, all writers come to this point: the point where the very project of writing itself, the very use of words, their bare existence, becomes the problem to be solved, the barrier to be busted through. Can I use words to destroy words? Can I use writing to lay bare the futility, the inherent weakness of these symbols, these marks, their inability to come anywhere near touching the essence of living? What else is left to try?

A committed primitivist—as opposed to someone like me, who is just prim-curious—would understand this dilemma, but, after listening to my anxieties, they would then patiently explain that there is, in fact, something else left to try. If writing is not the truth, can never be the truth, can only ever be a faint representation of it, then this is merely a function of a deeper problem. As primitivist philosopher John Zerzan explains, in paragraphs ironically dense with turgid academic prose, the ultimate source of our alienation from the rest of nature is language itself:

> To Levy-Bruhl, Durkheim and others, the cardinal and qualitative difference between the 'primitive mind' and ours is the primitive's lack of detachment in the moment of experience; 'the savage mind totalizes,' as Levi-Strauss put it. Of course we have long been instructed that this original unity was destined to crumble, that alienation is the province of being human: consciousness depends on it.
>
> In much the same sense that objectified time has been held to be essential to consciousness—Hegel called it 'the necessary alienation'—so has language, and equally falsely. Language may be properly considered the fundamental ideology, perhaps as deep a separation from the natural world as self-existent time. And if timelessness resolves the split between spontaneity and consciousness, language-lessness may be equally necessary.

Words, language, symbolic thought itself: is this the gauze which hangs between me and the world, the gauze which occasionally rips in part or sways in the wind, offering me a glimpse of unity between the picture and myself, but which never fully falls away? Is the gauze a product of my consciousness itself, of my forebrain, of my evolutionary heritage? Did growing up with *language* mean I would always feel disconnected? Is this what clumsily I try to break with my moves to the country, my attempted divorce from the Machine, my moments on the mountain or with the pen and notepad, and can I never break it until, yes, I lay down the pen, and not just the pen? Do I have to walk out there unarmed with ideas and representations of ideas before I can be part of the world again? How the hell could I possibly do that?

This is a life sentence with no possibility of probation.

A worldview like primitivism, while posing sometimes as a philosophy or even as politics, seems to me more like a psychological, even a spiritual, cry for help. It is a search for the source of Hegel's 'necessary alienation,' which it finds in our severance from a pre-civilized age of peaceful, artistic, egalitarian and perhaps matriarchal hunter-gatherers for which there is precious little actual evidence. But that's what makes it so attractive. Projecting your dreams or desires is easiest when you know little about the place, the person, or the time onto which you are projecting. This is why it's so easy to romanticize Mesolithic hunter-gatherers, 25th century Mars-dwelling immortals, and that woman you saw briefly across a bar who flashed you an amazing smile and then left before you could pluck up the courage to even ask her name.

Primitivism is dangerous for me because it plays into a pre-existing tendency of mine—a tendency which, judging by human history, I share with plenty of others—which is to look backwards in search of a breaking point: the moment at which we stepped from the True Path. I spent years doing this, and sometimes I still do it. *When did it all go wrong?* The Industrial Revolution. Fossil fuels. Modernity. The Enlightenment. Capitalism. Science.

Agriculture. Hunting. Fire. Language. Symbolic thought. Coming down from the trees. Crawling up onto the land. Soon enough you find yourself obliquely or not-so-obliquely espousing the notion of Original Sin: *the poison is in us, the poison is us. It is how we think. It is our very minds.* Or, as the novelist William Golding put it, more simply: 'The Fall is thought.'

I've been on both sides of this conversation over the years: I've argued the primitivist case and opposed it, depending on who I was talking to. I'm like that: pushed easily into the opposing camp when I hear someone expressing a strong opinion. It's easy to see the flaws in someone else's ideological positioning, and then it's logical to argue with them if you're the sort of person who is drawn to arguing or can be led to believe that it can ever resolve anything at all. After a while, this grinds you down enough that you can see the flaws in your own ideological positioning too, which in turn leads you to realize the absurdity of any kind of ideological positioning, and the next thing you know you're reading Camus on the beach and you've stopped thinking about the Stone Age entirely. For a while. But not for long enough.

26.

At this point, even as they abandon me, or force me to fall silent, I feel like making a stand for words. I feel like making a stand for books, for writing, for the abstract and the conceptual. I feel like making a stand for the European mind. Maybe Eros and Psyche are divorced now, and painfully. Maybe they don't speak anymore, maybe they fight over custody of the kids. Maybe I can't hear the old echoes, maybe the flaming hoop is broken and doused, but this is where I am and who I am. Here

I stand, a child of modernity, a boy from the post-war suburbs of England, adrift in an Irish fieldscape as the echoes float by. The echoes are all I have. What can I make of them, and how do I start?

D. H. Lawrence, deep into his 'savage pilgrimage' in New Mexico, wrote an essay in 1922, 'Indians and an Englishman,' in which he concluded that, however much he might yearn to sit around that tribal fire, he was separated from it by his modernity as surely as Adam and Eve were separated from Eden:

> *I don't want to live again the tribal mysteries my blood has lived long since. I don't want to know as I have known, in the tribal exclusiveness. But every drop of me trembles still alive to the old sound, every thread in my body quivers to the frenzy of the old mystery. I know my derivation. I was born of no virgin, of no Holy Ghost. Ah, no, these old men telling the tribal tale were my fathers.*

Ah, Lawrence! Where have all the writers like him gone? Stupid question: there were never any other writers like him. But I mean to say: why is it so shameful now to *burn* the way that he did? I suppose it was shameful then too, and that's why he was made to eat shit all his life and after it by magistrates and judges and defenders of public morals and cowards hiding behind ideologies and minnowy critics mired in post-whatever theory. Working class, openly passionate, proudly masculine, in love with the feminine, anti-modern, anti-egalitarian: Lawrence never stood a chance. He knew that modern humans were animals who acted like animals and he knew we were ashamed of it and he urged us, instead, to be ashamed of the civilization that made us feel that way. He knew the animal would outlast the Machine and he knew that the Earth was alive. *Of course. Of course.* He could feel the old mystery quivering in every thread of his body and he was bold and suicidal enough to say so to an audience of frightened 20th century cynics and they never let him forget it. Lawrence grew up, as we all grow up, in a Machine world in which the feted artists are the ones prepared to act and talk and create like good little well-behaved Machine people, using the right words to say the right things to the right audiences in the right way for the right outcome. They were never going to hear what he had to say, because what he had to say exposed what they really were.

Enough of this. I could do it all day: defending Lawrence and those writers almost-like-him against the ruling robot people. I ought to calm down. I don't think it's good for me to do it in anything other than short, concentrated bursts. It makes me itch and fidget and start to rage. Plus, whenever I think of Lawrence these days I'm aware that I have now reached the age he was— 44—when he died, and thinking about this will start me off on a *what the hell have I ever done that even approaches what he did?* train of thought, or a *when was I ever half as brave as he was?* session, and then it's time to start drinking. I can't start drinking now. All the wine's gone.

Lawrence, sitting with those Indians in New Mexico, felt too that he stood 'on the far edge of their firelight'; that something in him meant he could never sit comfortably around that campfire, even if he wanted to. He was 'neither denied nor accepted,' he wrote, but he was always a few paces outside. The old path wasn't walkable for him. The songlines wouldn't sing. 'My way is my own, old red father,' he concluded. 'I can't cluster at the drum any more.'

I have to feel the same; I do. But for a society which has severed itself from the past, what remains? In the Machine world, amongst the robot people, where is life to be found? Where is my indigeneity, who are my ancestors, what is our lost place and who will tell us its stories?

The words. The writing.

'In Western Civilization,' says the poet Gary Snyder, 'our elders are books.' Books pass on our stories. Books carry the forbidden knowledge and the true. Books are weird things, inhuman things, abstract things, but they are gateways, at their best, to the world to which the drum and the fire and the sweat lodge used to take us. The Otherworld. At her best, the writer is a shaman, a priestess, a summoner.

'The writer knows his field,' writes Annie Dillard. 'In writing, he can push the edges. Beyond this limit, here, the reader must recoil. Reason balks, poetry snaps; some madness enters, or strain. Now courageously and carefully, can he enlarge it, can he nudge the bounds? And enclose what wild power?'

27.

Reason, implies Dillard, is not enough in our business. Milan Kundera agrees. 'Imagination,' he writes, 'freed from the control of reason and from concern for verisimilitude, ventures into landscapes inaccessible to rational thought.' As in the fire ceremony, as in the rite of passage, something older and more ragged, more dangerous too, is invited into the circle. No writer who imagines that reason, argument, logic or the rational presentation of well-researched facts will do their job for them will ever enclose that wild power.

Writing, suggests Dillard, is the disciplined pursuit of unreason, the willful, controlled enclosure of magic by words. That's when it works; that's when you've hit it. You always know. Then, you are a wizard. You have never felt more alive than when that sentence does its job; when the beast can never escape from the words you have wrapped it in. When the trap is sprung.

This: this is what I have lived for.

We judge writers either as teachers, storytellers, or enchanters, suggested Vladimir Nabokov, but it is the enchanter who out-lasts time. Outlasting time: that's what we're in the business of, all of us. Writing is the pursuit of immortality. As long as this book sits on a shelf somewhere in the British Library, even if no one withdraws it for a hundred years—as long as it's there, I can never die. I know, it's terrible. Arrogant, egocentric, the very opposite of wisdom. But it's true.

28.

Or is it? That last paragraph was nicely self-effacing, but actually the pursuit of immortality is a side-effect of writing, not its aim or purpose. Nobody would spend their life on words if the only benefit they got was that somebody might read them after they were under the ground. Some of us tell ourselves that we write not for the present but for posterity—usually when no one is buying our books—but it's not what pumps the blood through the writing hand.

Why write? Rainer Maria Rilke, the German language's great-est modern poet, took his young protégé Franz Kappus to task in 1903 on this question. Stop worrying about whether 'your poems are good poems,' Rilke instructed him. Stop sending them off to magazine editors and feeling like a failure when they reject them. Stop asking the world's opinion. The world's opinion has nothing to do with why you do this:

> *You must seek for whatever it is that obliges you to write. You must discover if its roots reach down to the very depths of your heart. You must confess to yourself whether you would truly die if writing were forbidden to you. This above all: ask yourself in the night, in your most silent hour — Must I write? If there is an affirmative reply, if you can simply and starkly answer 'I must' to that grave question, then you will need to construct your life according to that necessity.*

The only reason to write is because you *can't not write*; because something sharp and heated is pushing you through. We write, I write, because of life's brevity and the need to blaze. Rilke's poetry blazed because he pointed himself at it like a spear and everything else fell away. He blazed because he built his life around words, until it ended at the age of just 51. If I die at 51 I have another seven years of life left. What am I going to do with them? How am I going to blaze? I've been asking myself that question, neurotically, since I was about 21. It adds a terrible, tiring urgency to life.

But this is the heat from which words are born. Nobody writes for money, power, fame, or sex, none of which writing is likely to get you anywhere near, at least for long. It's the blazing—the burning. It's the intensity of *being*: of love, of sorrow, joy, grief, brokenness, loss. It's the aching of all that is short and will soon be washed away. You have your one, brief, tiny life. You have your pen. Can you convey the heat of it? The way that every cell burns with the true light when you realize, in some tremendous moment—some kiss, some death, some echo across a midnight lake—the high, thin, oxygenless truth of *being here*? Of living? Can you get even a sliver of that onto a page? That is what you came for. Everything else is flotsam. Everything else can be shrugged away on the tide. Get it down. Get it down. Capture it. There is nothing else.

29.

Late May. I am in the field, scything the grass and the docks down. I am mowing shirtless in the rain and I remember why I came here and suddenly, in an instant and just for an instant, I am *here*. I am nowhere else. I am the field and the motion of the scythe and the falling of the rain and the movement of the muscles in my back and shoulders, the sideways motion of my stiff hips and I think nothing at all. I just mow. I just move. I just am. For a moment, I just *am*.

Sometimes, when you least expect it, you are given a gift.

30.

One man went to mow a meadow. One man and his dog. And as the man shuffled slowly forwards, slicing the dock with his scythe blade and wondering if it was time to sharpen it again, one man suddenly realized this: that however many words he used up trying to explain himself, none would ever fall anywhere near the mark because there was no mark to aim at. Everything the man did, all of his actions and the stated reasons for all of his actions, all this was like steam rising from the boiling lake of his unconscious, and he had no idea what the heat source was. All the pulls and pushes, the justifications and opinions, the thoughts and actions were waves on top of deep, dark waters and he would never see into the depths of what lived down there or swam through. Nothing in the universe could ever be explained or written. All the words were blowing away like vapor. *One, two, three. Answer!* But the blade cut easily through the dock stems and now the rain was coming in again, always from the west.

31.

This move from fire to water: it is real for us all, I think, and it is hard. Back around the campfire there would be ceremonies, rites of passage, there would be people to hold you, there would be mythic containers for the journey. In our culture, if we have a culture, we have no rites of passage because we don't understand transitions and we are terrified of age and death. In our culture we don't grow up. Parents act like children, 60-year-olds dress like 20-year-olds, men are boys forever. Capitalist consumer culture renders us perpetually adolescent, stuck behind a door we don't know how to open. It sells excuses like the Church once sold indulgences, and the stink of corruption is just as rank.

It has taken me a long time—pages and pages, thousands of words—to begin to understand what is happening to me and to understand that I can't stop it happening, that my only choice is to sit through it, to walk through the wood one step at a time without pretending I know where I'm going. I don't know where I am going. I think that's the point. I think that's the challenge. My words have lifted off me and away, up into the night canopy and I am walking on now, silent and alone. One step at a time. It has to be enough, because it is all there is.

Now I can feel the fire and the water rush against each other, feel the hissing fog of steam that is born from the meeting. I am moving into water time but part of me is still burning. Who wants their fire extinguished? What fire wants to die down before its time? I am not ready. I am not ready!

But the heat escapes through tiny cracks and the fire rages upwards, burns through the beams to get where it needs to be, brings the building down. I don't know what will be left of me after this burning. I have no idea at all.

32.

And so, I am stuck. Lost for words and with only half a book on my hands. What does a writer do when he discovers that writing is part of the problem? He writes differently

or he stops writing.

I know what the silence demands of me.

You build up a career, even if a career was the last thing on your mind, even if you have always hated careers and run from them, you end up with one and then people think they know what you do and they ask you to keep doing it, and you have to earn a living and so you keep doing it and anyway you enjoy it, it's fine really, it's good. But then something, just a tiny thing, something small, invisible even, gets *stuck*. Something lodges somewhere in

the great firmament of yourself and it stays there and it itches.
It just keeps itching.

You know what it wants.

But I can't walk away. Not yet. Something made me write this.
Something called it into being. Words don't just drop out of
the sky, they have to be formed, and books too. Books are like
people: they come from somewhere and they have to belong
somewhere and they want something, though you don't always
know what it is.

I have to keep going.

33.

The poet W. S. Graham referred to whatever power it is that
lives behind and activates words as 'the beast in the space.' In
his poem of the same name, he described what it did to him
whenever it approached, demanding verse:

> The beast that lives on silence takes
> Its bite out of either side.
> It pads and sniffs between us. Now
> It comes and laps my meaning up.

This beast is a dangerous animal, says Graham, though not mali-
cious. Just hungry; always hungry. The act of writing sends the
beast across the space from the writer to the reader. If the writer
has done his job properly, the beast is now the reader's problem.
'Give him food,' Graham advises his readers, in the final lines.
Be respectful, be cautious. Keep the beast happy:

He means neither
Well or ill towards you. Above
All, shut up. Give him your love.

34.

If not writing, then what?

Being, I suppose. But being is harder. Harder than writing, and more boring. In my 20s, I wanted to be Bruce Chatwin, or some version of the Romantic traveler. I would escape my suburban life and my suburban mind, and I would see and record the world, I would write its beauty out. But because I never really knew even the small things which I skimmed over and ran from, whenever I did get away I would find myself inescapable. I could travel anywhere but I would take the gauze with me, because I was not paying attention to what I was running from, or where I had been, or what I was carrying.

Here, I could do this with the land I live on, and with my life. I know this, because I have found myself doing it—treating the place like a backdrop or a writing exercise. I could pour myself into the land this way, but the land would not receive me. I could tell my story in big letters, in primary colors and maybe publish it to some acclaim but you would be unsatisfied and I would be lying because no painter who can't do detail is ever any good at all. We can all do broad brushstrokes. I could make this place a backdrop for some grand thesis or I could *pay attention*, to it, and to myself in it. I could *really* watch, not assuming that, before I even start, I will receive an answer which will lead my latest book to a satisfying conclusion.

What if there are no satisfying conclusions? What if there is only the great flaming hoop and us spinning inside it? No end and no knowing. What if I don't know the person who writes all this down, or the place he wanders in, because I have skipped over what I thought were the boring bits of the story?

35.

We bought a small house and two and a half acres of land here from people we didn't know. Five years before that, those people had bought the same place from a person they didn't know. Perhaps in the meantime the place had risen or fallen in notional value, but it remained a resource: an area of land over which ownership could be expressed, a claim staked. You buy a place, you live in it for a while, you sell it, you move on. This is how I was brought up: where I come from, we call it the 'housing ladder,' it's about buying, doing up, and selling on at a profit, and it has by this point in history pretty comprehensively screwed our children's future.

Above all, it is about being *temporary*. A temporary person, always moving on. Since I have lived here I have come to understand, with a startling clarity, how different I might have been as a human being, how differently I would look at the world, if I had inherited this land from my parents and expected to hand it on to my children. Maybe that is the remains of our indigeneity. Just staying put. At least since the development of agriculture, this would have been how the majority of humans saw their homes. Not as resources to be exploited or temporarily enjoyed, but as inheritances to be cared for and passed on. I imagine how I would feel about this land if I'd been passed it by my mother and father, if I'd grown up on it with them, if it had been constructed by their hands and my memories. And I think about how much more carefully perhaps I would nurture it, how much more pride I would have in it, how much more love I could afford to give it if I knew that one day it would be my children's, and that they would inherit their own memories from it. That one day, after Jyoti and I are gone, Leela and Jeevan, as adults, might sit on a bench by the pond they once watched us dig, under the mature trees they helped us plant as children, and watch the frogs jumping as they jump now. I would have my connection across time then, my mooring in a place, I would be a link in a long chain and there would be a meaning in my life that is not here now. Would that not be a beautiful thing?

It would be. That's the stuff of a good human life, and I want it, but with conditions. I want to be in a place, but I want to be able, simultaneously, to write my way out of it. When I was younger, writing was my form of escape. To escape from everything the world loaded onto me, to go somewhere else, to be free there. To run upstairs, away from the family gathering or the family argument, to sit in my bedroom and scribble. All my young writing, before I was in my mid-30s, was about escape. Since then it's been about what the Ancient Greeks called *Nostos*—homecoming. I thought that was a simple pattern and a natural one. Young man is fire, older man is water. It's the oldest of old patterns. I was starting to enjoy it, until the cracks appeared.

But it occurs to me now that wanting to root yourself somewhere can also be a form of escape. As a young man, running away from stability and solidity towards adventure and excitement is pretty standard behavior, but you can't keep it up forever. I thought that the next step was to settle down and dig in and gain some contentment from stillness and rootedness. But when I look back at how I have written about this over the last several years I can see only now—and how did it take me this long?—that wanting to be rooted is also a search for escape, only this time a different kind of escape. Wanting a stable home on an unchanging plot of land is a search for stability, and that in turn is a search for freedom from the whirling, unmoored, unpredictable reality of living inside a single human mind that cannot and will not ever stop seeking, asking questions, racing across the skies like the winds race. I wanted, perhaps more than is healthy, for this place to protect me. I wanted this plot to be the answer. And it wasn't, because if there is an answer—if there is ever an answer to anything—it is never to be found outside.

Wanting to be pulled down to earth, into water, is a desire to escape from the fire. It is a desire no longer to be burned by the world, or by yourself. But what if you can never escape the fire?

What if you are the fire?

Nostos is the theme of all 24 books of Homer's *The Odyssey*. And when Odysseus finally arrives back in Ithaca, after 20 years of exile, after fighting off the Cyclops and the witch-goddess Circe, after being pursued and wrecked by Poseidon, after negotiating Scylla and Charybdis, after losing so many men, after being shipwrecked and drugged and seduced and nearly destroyed—when he finally arrives back to the green shores of Ithaca,

then the real work starts.

36.

This urge to run and at the same time to belong: how does it fit together? Only in the way that all the impulses contained within our individual skins fit together, which is to say, they don't. Really, the notion of 'fitting together' is almost comical. Nothing we do fits with anything else, if by 'fits' we mean 'makes up some kind of cohesive whole.' Being a grown-up is the business of integrating our chaotic multitudes. We all want 17 contradictory things at once, and only puritans and ideologues have ever believed otherwise.

So I can tell myself that I am still looking for my lost indigeneity, and it's not an untrue story, but the reality of this drive is probably only to be found down at the bottom of that boiling lake, where my conscious mind can never go. Perhaps I just have to ride it out, like the early Christian monks rode out the winter storms in their tiny stone oratories on the Atlantic seaboard of this old green island. But when do you cling to the rock, and when do you let go and trust the weather? What does deliverance look like?

Place. Culture. Identity. Belonging. They are entwined things, beautiful things, powerful, deep, and necessary things, toxic things, limiting things, primitive things. I have long believed they are the stock at the base of the human soup, but what is the price I pay for believing things like that? At its worst, it is a head always turned to the past, where this phantom 'belonging' might once have been found: to the lost Garden, the primitivist Eden where all was well. But there is no past, never, and no future, only this ongoing moment, only this *now*, and if I can't belong to it here, now, I can't belong to anything.

The search is the thing and the search is the danger, the search is what makes you ludicrous if you never find and never learn; learn that the desire to belong and the refusal to belong might be entwined too. Learn that you can get stuck in the search. Patrick Kavanagh, peasant poet of Monaghan, knew the price well:

Culture is always something that was,
Something pedants can measure,
Skull of bard, thigh of chief,
Depth of dried-up river.
Shall we be thus for ever?
Shall we be thus for ever?

Kavanagh's poiesis was a process of shedding skins, of casting off personas, of dropping notions and ideas and poses and beliefs until he was, by the end of his life, stripped down to bare soil. He began as a poet in 1930s Ireland by hymning his rural peasant upbringing for an urbane Dublin audience. Later, in reaction to their comfortable applause—for Kavanagh, too, couldn't abide comfort or acceptance for long—he took to angrily deconstructing that same upbringing, using his poetry to rub his readers' noses in the hardship of rural life, most famously in his famine-poem *The Great Hunger.*

The hungry fiend
Screams the apocalypse of clay
In every corner of this land.

But he didn't stop there. In stripping away the Romance of the soil, he found himself reacting against the poetic nationalism which was still so predominant across Ireland. Kavanagh set himself up in opposition to the poetic vision of W. B. Yeats, he of the grand house and the Ascendancy and the faeries and the 'indomitable Irishry.' Kavanagh opposed Yeats' nationalism with his own poetic project: parochialism. Nationalism, he said, was false and totalizing: the Irish nation was a constructed political fiction and literary 'Irishness' was thus 'a form of anti-art.'

Kavanagh's parochialism offered instead a celebration of a proud local particularity. A parochial writer, he said, was 'never in any doubt about the social and artistic validity of his parish.' Poetic reality, all lived reality, was to be found under the poet's feet. All else was fiction or grandstanding. If you couldn't see it or really know it, you shouldn't write about it. One small piece of earth: that was all a man needed, and all a poet needed too. It had ever been thus. 'I made the *Iliad* from such a local row,' he has Homer say in one of his poems. 'Gods make their own importance.'

But Kavanagh couldn't settle onto his plateau either. His parochialism might have been a good place for a poet to raise a flag, a sound and distinctive and marketable manifesto to build a career on, but he didn't stop moving even when he reached the dark wood. Soon he had grown dissatisfied with parochialism too, dissatisfied with his need to identify stances and projects and positions. Poets, he concluded, and artists in general, should avoid positions and manifestoes the same way they avoid gainful employment. Polemicism, to Kavanagh, was now the enemy of art. In that mood, he repudiated *The Great Hunger*, still his most famous poem, which he now saw as a politicized, and therefore dishonest, piece of writing. 'A true poet is selfish and implacable,' he declared. 'A poet merely states the position and does not care whether his words change anything or not.'

Kavanagh knew that by rejecting what he referred to as 'the tragic thing'—the poetry of rural misery and hardship, the story that a certain audience wanted to be told—he was potentially committing commercial and critical suicide. He knew what people wanted from him, and what he represented to them. 'But I lost my messianic compulsion,' he explained. 'I sat on the bank of the Grand Canal in the summer of 1955 and let the water lap idly on the shores of my mind. My purpose in life was to have no purpose.'

I wonder what that feels like. To have no purpose. I can see the attraction. Sometimes I would like to stop giving a shit about anything. I would like to stop work on all my construction projects. I would like to retire. I would love to be a historyless person, a placeless person, unclaimed by the past, by the skulls and thighs, and by the future, by the causes and factions. No place, no name, no home, no past, no future. That's freedom.

But isn't it also death?

37.

The weight of running, the weight of staying, maybe they balance out in the end. I wonder if they are like weights on each side of a balance. I wonder if to encompass, to contain, both is as normal as the sea. Why would I imagine that the landscape inside me would be smooth and level and manageable like some suburban lawn and not heaving with ragged, unending conflict like a torrent in a forest gully, bright with ever-coming rain?

Wanting to run, wanting to stay—are they waves in the same ocean? Or, as Galway Kinnell sees them, the two movements of a windscreen wiper—run / stay / run / stay. You are not the first and will not be the last who will never be able to choose:

> *The windshield wipers wipe, homesickness one way, wander-*
> *lust the other, back and forth.*
> *This happened to your father and to you, Galway—sick to*
> *stay, longing to come up against the ends of the earth,*
> *and climb over.*

38

In the Kavanagh-versus-Yeats battle, I try to remain neutral. I like having them both in my life and on my side. Yeats appeals to my Romantic side, which is not really a side, more of a core. He speaks to the side of me which paints big pictures, which sets out notions, which listens to the winds and sees spirits in the hedges. Kavanagh appeals to my anti-messianic aspect, the wanderer, the kicker-against-everything, the soul that drifts like the clouds and sticks to nothing at all.

My inner Kavanagh regularly battles with my inner Yeats. My inner Kavanagh is bloody-minded and self-destructive. It wants to strip away the world's delusions and my own, detach from all notions, be joyful, have fun and do good work and screw the rest. My inner Yeats wants to go hunting for wandering Aengus in the Burren at dusk, prefers the inner flame to the outer ashes and is constantly disappointed that his imagined world is nothing like the real one.

Coming here has been a good lesson in the limits of Romanticism, and that has been good for me. It's easy to romanticize farming until you live among farmers, just as it's easy to romanticize nature until you have to feed yourself. Once you have to clear the rats from your compost heap and the slugs from your raised beds, once you have to protect your young apples from starlings and your newly-planted asparagus from rooks, once you have to build a 200-yard fence to keep the fluffy bunnies away from your beans, then you begin to identify less with Peter Rabbit and more with Mr McGregor. I have found that I actively enjoy excavating this side of myself. It's the side of me that has to make a living and feed my kids, even if rabbits and starlings get in the way. It's the side of me that hangs around in the farm supply shop nodding approvingly at rat traps and thinking about buying a shotgun. My Romantic side flowers and roars out when I spend a lot of time with words. The more time I spend building fences and topping docks, the more Yeats retreats into his tower. Did he ever build a fence? I don't know, but I doubt it.

But I love Yeats, all the more so because he is increasingly as unfashionable as Lawrence amongst the apostles of techno-conformity, and for many of the same reasons. Yeats is an anti-Machine poet, a man tuned to the old mysteries. A Machine age, dominated by those who can most loudly express their aggressive commitment to a totalizing progress, can do nothing but mock him. I need Yeats in my life, and I need Kavanagh too, for balance. I need R. S. Thomas for my dose of dark Welsh mysticism, Dylan Thomas for alcoholic visions, Edward Thomas for nostalgic English pastoral. I need Neruda and Dickinson, Wordsworth and Rilke, Szymborska and Graves, all squabbling away inside me as I net the asparagus bed against the rooks and the blackbirds.

Words, words, words. But beneath the symbols, something stirs.

39.

For the first 20 years of my life, my primary influence—or, rather, my most dominating and direct influence—was a self-made father who channeled me in the same direction he had channeled himself, which is to say in the direction of somebody who never stopped pushing towards goals, somebody who had something to escape from, somebody for whom movement was not a means to an end but simply an end. I was brought up to push beyond, never to look down, never to stop moving.

For the next 20 years of my life, I took this ongoing movement and applied it to the entire world. As a kid, I'd felt most at
peace on mountains, in woods, in fields—away from the town,
the house, the ongoing movement and all of the pressure that
went with the ongoing movement. I'd loved animals and birds
and the still of soft-flowing streams. Then I went to university,
I discovered environmental activism, my family strictures fell
away, I met people with dreadlocks who hated The System and
could show me how to chain myself to things to stop green
and peaceful places like the ones I had been formed by being
bulldozed for houses and roads. You start with the houses and
roads and then you start to think about the things that power the
houses and roads and the forces that create the need for them
and before you know it you're against capitalism, climate change,
the entire industrial economy and everything humans have ever
done since they discovered fire or planted seeds or dug the first
seam of coal.

At this point, the world is still as simple as it was when my
dad taught me that there were winners and losers and I had to
choose which I would be, only this time there are Earth Killers
and Earth Protectors and which one are you, whose side are you
on? And all of this is exciting and true and real and necessary
and now the planet, the world, *everything*, needs to be saved, by
me and a few true others and this is urgent, it must happen *now*,
there is no time to lose, it must happen now and

and

and it is impossible.

The resulting collapse of will and hope is a necessary stage in the
journey towards maturity, I think now, and I'm sure the old stories would have something to say about it. Still, it hurts. I think

it hurt me for years longer than I admitted it. For years, I wrote about this collapse, tried to dig into the feelings that welled up from it, tried to explore the meaning of living in a world whose doom is delineated in parts per million of carbon and glacial melt and extinction rates. It consumed me for years, but it was a heavy weight to carry; heavier than I would admit to. All that darkness. It was a strange kind of literary therapy. And the work turned into grief work, it turned into growth work, it turned into a burden, in the end, and it sat on my shoulders and it weighed me down and I didn't even know it. And then one day, one day a few months ago, the day I began writing this book, the day I sat up until 2 a.m. in a college bedroom far from home, beginning this book before I even knew what I was beginning—that day, suddenly, for no reason that I have yet been able to understand, all the weight just slid away.

40.

If I believed for too long that the world was controllable—that we could perfect it if we all just worked hard enough—it was an idea I got from my father; the primary idea he drove into me as a child. It is an idea that can serve if you remember it is just that—an idea. If you mistake the map for the territory, though—if you start to believe that reality will bend to your will if you just grip it hard enough—then you are asking for trouble.

My dad was the kind of man who was brought up like this by his dad, who was also that kind of man, I think. There are too many men like this in the world. He was the kind of man whose own father made it clear to him from a young age that he was a failure who would never amount to anything. He was the kind of man who spent the next 40 years advancing up the ladder from apprentice to company director to prove his dad wrong but who, I think, must always have felt like a scared child somewhere inside and who dealt with this by treating everyone else in the world like children also. He walked through the world carving a sharp path. Everyone would fall before him. Everyone would obey him, especially his family, and when they didn't there would be hell to pay. The explosions that resulted when any of us—especially my mum—did not follow his instructions are some of my most reliable childhood memories. Duck, or run for cover: these were your choices.

This is a partial picture, and therefore an unfair one. If a dozen people live inside me, if a hundred do, then the same would have been true for him. He could be kind, and he could be fun. He spent time with his children and supported his family. He did the things dads are supposed to do, or some of them. He tried.

But underneath everything, always, was this rage and this need for control. I idolized my dad as a small boy, because that's what small boys do. Then, at some later stage, probably as a young teenager, after years of exposure to his controlling aggression, I started to look at him the way Bruce Springsteen looked at his father in his song *Independence Day*, and I made the same vow: *they ain't gonna do to me what I watched them do to you.*

Them? My dad had found his place in the world of business, a world which matched his own outlook on life and justified it: you were strong or weak, you won or lost and you had to make sure you were on the right side of the fence. My dad was always on the right side of the fence, the side in which he was a winner. In my dad's newfound world, in which he came of age as Thatcherism swept all before it, everything came second to profit, to setting targets and meeting them, and this brought out the worst in him and dissolved the best.

I was not going to be eaten this way. I was not going to have my heart eaten this way. I despised the values of the world I had seen him grow into and promote. And so I grew up and became an angry anti-capitalist student, much to my dad's horror—which was half the point, I suppose—and then wrote two books about how much I hated corporations and the world of business and all the values they promoted, which were and are seeping into every crack in my society, making everything in life the shape of an open-plan office full of middle managers in nylon trousers whose souls died years back on the M25.

Money, money money! says Mellors the gamekeeper to Lady Chatterley as they lie in his bed in the bluebell wood. *All the modern lot get their real kick out of killing the old human feeling out of a man.*

Those were the days in which I made my words serve my cause, a cause which took in everything in the whole world. I would make the whole world better with my words, I would show that it could be made better. Those were the days when the external landscape represented my internal landscape and taking on one meant taking on the other. If I could help stick it to Monsanto or the World Trade Organization, it would represent one great big *fuck you* to my dad and all of his values. They ain't gonna do to me what I watched them do to you, *Dad.*

41.

It was never that simple, of course. Nothing is ever that simple. As soon as you think you have identified a cause or a reason for your actions or feelings, it immediately starts to look glib, simplistic, narrow. Events can't explain everything. Maybe they can't explain anything. People are mostly inexplicable, I think now, which is maybe another reason I find it so hard to write about them.

In the end, you can only ever live with the things which make you. There is no guarantee that you will ever understand them. Life is not a puzzle to be solved. In one way or another, I suppose, these things go on in every life, in every household, all the time. They go on within each of us, all the time. This is the stuff of life. We live through it, and then it lives through us and none of it makes for a story with a comfortable moral thread or any consistent characters at all.

42.

In 2008, after several years in which none of his plans went right, in which all his control systems broke down, in which nobody would obey him anymore, in which none of his rages produced results, my dad took his own life. 'Took his own life' is what we are supposed to say now, I recently learned, 'suicide' having been designated by somebody or other as offensive and problematic. Still, *suicide* is a better word: it's harder, less euphemistic. My dad decided that death was better than humiliation and so he took to the motorway without a seatbelt and looked for something to stop him. When I try to remember how I felt when I heard this news, it's hard to recall the sensation. I think I felt empty, or relieved, or empty and relieved, or something like that. I felt guilty, too, and still do sometimes. I felt I should have been there with him to prevent it. But I also felt like something inevitable had happened. I didn't feel sadness. I wonder about that.

Despite everything, I have always wanted to be fair to my dad, who can't now answer back. Even having exposed him like this, in a way he would have hated and been shamed by, I still find myself wanting to be fair to him. It's why I resisted writing about this for 10 years, even though writing things down is my impulsive reaction to every single thing in my life. I wanted to keep it out of the public eye because—well, why? Because it's nobody else's business, for starters. But then writers are in the business of what is nobody else's business. What right do I have? What right did he have?

The other reason, though: everybody fucks up. I can look back and trace the wrong turnings that my dad made. He was human. He got it wrong, and then wrong again, but along the way he got things right too. I could tell you that I had some horrible, abusive childhood and maybe that would sell more books, but it wouldn't be true. My childhood was fine, mostly. Sometimes pressured, and with the constant background hum of my dad's need for control, but I had plenty of good times, and both my parents loved me. Everything seemed normal. That's what 'normal' is for. It's a word we use to paint over the cracks in what we fail to live with.

Yet now I find that, like some slow-spreading oil slick eating up a living ocean, the end of my father's life has become more real to me than the way he lived it, and the horrors which came at the end—horrors I will still not write about—have become more vivid across time than any of the good things he gave me. I can't help feel downcast about this. It feels like a failure. I wonder if it is his failure or mine.

In the end, all my dad's wrong turnings took him so deep into the wood that he could never find his way out and he died alone there, lost and raging. I enjoy judging him for this, sometimes. It makes me feel strong and righteous and powerful. It draws a line between us, and I am not a boy anymore when I am behind it. He can't touch me here. Ha ha! Fuck you, Dad!

But it could have been me. It could have been you. Maybe one day it will be. Mercy. Mercy.

43.

There's a fear, a fear or a promise, that sits with perhaps anyone whose parent dies by suicide: that some things are handed down. That some ghost haunts your line, and that now it's done with your father, now it has had its way with him, it will turn its sights on you. That you look in the mirror and see your father's face and one day you will see more than that. And you, man—well, you're a writer, and we all know how writers die. The good ones anyway. The Romantic ones. This is how they show they are serious.

And there's the secret: that suicide, sometimes, is thrilling. That suicide, sometimes, is tempting, appropriate to the moment. That sometimes it seems like destiny. And these are the words whispered in your ear some restless night, when the moon is up and on the fields and some sharp energy fills you like the scent of tarragon, and something is singing far off in the trees:

You're next.

The poet Tony Hoagland, writing about the attraction of suicide, concludes that 'though I would still like to jump off a high
bridge / At midnight' to do so would represent a 'serious ingrat-
itude.' And anyway, he asks, 'Who has clothes nice enough to be
caught dead in?'

> *Not me. You stay alive you stupid asshole*
> *Because you haven't been excused,*
>
> *You haven't finished though it takes a mulish stubbornness*
> *To chew this food.*
>
> *It is a stone, is an inconvenience, it is an innocence,*
> *And I turn against it like a record*
>
> *Turns against the needle*
> *That makes it play.*

45.

My dad would identify what he wanted, and then he would go
and get it, and anyone in his way would be burned unless they
helped him on his journey or stood aside. I am not like this. I am
disappointingly weak in this way. I like to keep people happy.
I am more likely to apologize than to stand up for myself in any
given situation.

With one exception: the writing. For my writing I have sacrificed
relationships, money, security and sometimes my own health,
both mental and physical. I can give up almost anything else in

my life, but not the words, which is why what is happening to me now is so disturbing.

I know about my tendency to do this. I know it can consume me, and so for years I have tried instead to bury it. I have tried to bury it under land, work, family, children, marriage, ideas, theories, politics, manifestoes, organizations. I do not want to be the kind of writer who causes pain to those around him. 'When a writer is born into a family,' said the poet Czesław Miłosz, famously, 'the family is finished.' I used to object to this notion on principle. Since when did being a writer give someone *carte blanche* to be a shit, I wanted to know? How could writing be that important? In the end, they're only words.

Right?

That was what I wanted to believe, because I wanted to believe that my words were under my control and not the other way around. I wanted to believe that words were my tools, my instruments. I wanted to believe that I was the surgeon, but it was never true. When the writing I was doing was the real thing I was always the instrument, however blunt or rusty. And so I came here and I tried to bury my words and all their power, to hold them under, to fence them in on this plateau under the Irish sky. I thought I'd done it this time. I really did. I thought it was under control. I was so confident that I even stopped thinking about it.

Then the words broke out again and ran wild across the hills, crying at night and snarling. It turns out that they will never be held under. Do they want more than I was prepared to give? Are those gods hungry again? Do they want another sacrifice?

Why am I writing so much about gods? I have noticed this happening again and again, in almost everything I have written for years now. I can be writing a novel, an essay, a poem, on any subject, from any angle, and there they are, popping up from under every stone: gods. Strange, old, gnarled, primeval gods. They manifest in every guise I can think of, and some I clearly didn't think of by myself. Where did they come from, all these gods, and why?

I grew up irreligious and argumentative and materially minded and then something, in my 40s, went to work on me. I said earlier that I sometimes feel I am being called. Now that I've written myself through this thing, whatever it is, that feeling is even clearer. But what does it mean? I don't know. What could be calling me? *I don't know.*

What I do know is that when you give your words permission to access that boiling lake, to dig down beneath the shores of reason, to look out at the terrible madness and beauty of the universe or into the Gorgon's eyes or down into the abyss, then you are in danger of unleashing something you can't control. It's like playing with a Ouija board, or visiting a cabin in the woods with your teenage friends in an American horror film. You muck about with these things at your peril. If you open those doors, you have to know how to close them again.

There are many different gods, of course, which is why it matters which one your words, or your life, are serving. Hermes— Mercury—god of writers, boundary crosser, emissary between worlds, bringer of instability, sometimes madness: Hermes will fuck with your head. Bacchus, on the other hand, will probably just show you a good time. If you open the door to Freya, goddess of love and poetry, you're going to get a whole different experience to the one you would get if Loki was standing on the other side, holding a cheap bottle of wine and insisting that a friend of a friend invited him to your party.

Loki used to fascinate me as a teenager, while I was going through a phase of listening to Black Sabbath and Iron Maiden and obsessing over Norse mythology (these things tend to go together). For a while I convinced myself that I was the reincarnation of some Viking from the northern fjords. I had this strange affinity with pine forests, which still remains, and it was enough to build my shaky case on.

Loki was the Viking trickster god. Every culture has some representation of his energy. Half-demon, half-divine, son of a giant, father to a wolf and a serpent, he causes trouble, and sometimes the trouble is big. Lies, betrayal, violence, murder: Loki has done it all. He hates the other gods and they hate him, but they know, too, that he can be useful to them in their own machinations. He is never to be trusted, should rightly be expelled or killed, but that never happens and never could, because the energy he brings to the party, the trouble he carries, is some essential part of being human. Loki challenges boundaries, breaks through encrusted ideas, brings the dirt and danger from the margins into the heart of the kingdom. He is always around somewhere in your life. You probably need to just accept it and give him some space. Make up a bed for him in the spare room. The worst thing to do would be to tell yourself he had left town and wouldn't be coming back.

In his book on tricksters and the role they play in creativity, Lewis Hyde suggests that mythological figures like Loki, who has an equivalent in many other cultures—Hermes to the

Greeks, Eshu to the Yoruba, Coyote to some Native American tribes—help to create and reinvigorate culture precisely through the act of destruction. The trickster breaks boundaries so that boundaries might be redrawn. The trickster gives settled, staid cultures and people what they don't know they need: renewal.

> *Creative mobility in this world requires, at crucial moments, the strategic erasure of ethical boundaries. They lose that mobility who cling to beauty, or who suffer from what the poet Czeslaw Milosz has called 'an attachment to ethics at the expense of the sacred.'*

The trickster, in other words, brings a tough message: *what you need might not be what you want*. Sometimes, you have to do the 'wrong' thing to stay alive. And the trickster won't be denied. He knows when you need to be broken open. You can run from him, but you know you can't hide.

The worst crime Loki ever committed was to kill the 'beautiful god' Baldur. Baldur, who was loved by all the gods in Asgard, began to have a series of dark dreams prophesying his own death. Fearful, his mother, Frigg, forced every living thing on Earth, from the largest giant down to the smallest beetle, to swear an oath that they would not harm him. But she left one thing out: a tiny mistletoe plant. Loki noticed. Loki fashioned a spear from mistletoe. Loki took the spear to the blind god Hother, and persuaded him to throw it at Baldur, who was killed.

Why did Loki do this? Because what you need isn't always what you want. Because too much beauty and too much peace, too many rules and too many plans, can kill the soul as surely as too much chaos. Because change will not be denied. Because, even in Asgard, there is no plateau. Because without the pain, there is only entertainment:

There is no way to suppress change, the story says, not even in heaven; there is only a choice between a way of living that allows constant, if gradual, alterations and a way of living that combines great control and cataclysmic upheavals. Those who panic and bind the trickster choose the latter path. It would be better to learn to play with him, better especially to develop styles (cultural, spiritual, artistic) that allow some commerce with accident, and some acceptance of the changes contingency will always engender.

But there is something else here, too. In many mythologies it is the trickster, in the service of his destructive urges, of his need to break boundaries and cause trouble, who invents the lie. While the other gods, or the other animals, speak the truth plainly from their allotted place in the cosmos, the trickster, who belongs nowhere, who has no place and no role, needs to rely on his cunning and his deceit to get by. In the service of this deceit, he seems to have invented the technology which allows humans to lie so consistently and effectively: language. And in the service of language: writing.

Is Loki the god of writers? No. The trickster can't be anyone's light. He is far too much trouble. I do not serve Loki. I have no interest in meeting him. I want him to stay away from me. But I have a feeling that it's too late now. Whether from the boiling lake or the mead halls of Asgard, Loki seems to have turned up at my door, and though I'm sure I didn't let him in, he's somehow ended up inside anyway, booted feet on the sofa, drinking my beer, smiling up at me in a way which somehow, though it's impossible to quite put your finger on, is not at all kind.

It's been a long time, he says. *Aren't you pleased to see me?*

47

In the classic of Chinese literature, *Journey to the West*, the trickster figure is an arrogant, impulsive, swaggering, immortal monkey. As Loki was finally chained by the gods to a rock until world's end for killing Baldur, so Monkey was imprisoned by the Buddha below a mountain for 500 years for challenging the will of Heaven. *Journey to the West* centers around Monkey's epic trip with the monk Xuanzang to retrieve a series of sacred texts from the Buddha himself at the summit of an Indian mountain.

It takes them nearly 100 chapters of adventuring to reach the Buddha's citadel, but when they do they are handed the sacred scriptures and begin their journey back. It is Monkey, the cunning one, who thinks to actually check what they have been given as they travel. He unrolls the scrolls, only to find they are entirely blank. The travelers return to the Buddha's citadel, where they berate him for his deceit. 'How dare you give us these blank scrolls?' they demand. 'Where's the wisdom to be found here? Give us the real thing!'

The Buddha smiles at them. 'Fine,' he says, handing them some written scrolls; 'take these home instead.' But really, he explains, there was no deceit involved:

> As a matter of fact, it is such blank scrolls as these that are the true scriptures. But I quite see that the people of China are too foolish and ignorant to believe this, so there is nothing for it but to give them copies with some writing on.

48.

Some books are day books and some are night books. My last
novel was written in the mornings, between 7 and lunch, almost
daily like a ritual, alone in my cabin in the field. Most of my
writing happens in the morning, when things are cleaner, lighter.
Morning writing can be planned, organized, edited, controlled.
But this book has come at night, when everything is less defined,
and when humans are smaller. It is 1:30 a.m. as I write this.
I don't usually write late at night, but this book will not come
in the day and I have learned not to ask it to. This book won't
come in steady doses, planned and controlled and monitored
and strategically edited-as-I-go. This book won't let me sketch it
out, rein it in, and when I try I can feel it dying, can literally feel
the collapse in my fingertips and in my chest and neck. These
words want to use me and I am not to resist. They come clawing
out at me when the moon is up and everything sleeps but the
foxes and they will not ask my permission. This work is night
work. I am to do as I am told.

49.

It's 2 a.m. now. I stand and walk to the back door and open it
and walk outside. The dog follows me out and we stand on the
grass together. High, light clouds scud under a haloed full moon.
I stand in my dressing gown, looking up. A full moon has always
been a holy thing to me. I stretch my arms up and around my
body, bend over and down, rescuing my muscles from hours of
sitting. Then I get down on my knees before the moon, and give
it the praise it deserves.

The budding trees are stark in the blue silence. A cow lows gently in a barn three fields away. A dog barks from the other side of the river. The air is cool but not cold on my chest. Somewhere off to my right, I hear a low, distant hum.

50.

It's night again, nearly midnight this time, and I'm sitting on the sofa, typing. I wonder at what comes when I do this. Usually my books are planned: I sketch out each chapter, make sure the pre-determined themes run through the book, that it has a clear narrative, that it rises and falls in the right places, that the end comes around again to meet with the beginning and the closure is satisfying. I make sure I say everything I want to say. I do my research and back up my arguments. I can't write unplanned, any more than I can work with a messy desk. I need order.

This time around though, I have done none of that. I sat after midnight in a strange bedroom in a college miles from home and I felt something descend upon me, I felt the Muse address me, and I just began to write what came. The poet Robert Graves believed that the Muse was not a writer's metaphor but a real figure, a White Goddess, the embodiment of the moon, 'a lovely, slender woman with a hooked nose, deathly pale face, lips red as rowan-berries, startlingly blue eyes and long fair hair.' Every 'true poet' since Homer, said Graves, has seen and recorded his experience of the Goddess. Graves doesn't say whether this iron law applies to female poets. His relationship to his Muse-Goddess always sounded like it might be more than strictly literary to me.

Still, this energy that descends, this sense of being given a task, of being a vessel for some mystery—this is real, and any writer will tell you about it if you ask them and they are in the mood to talk about their writing, which most writers rarely are. Is it a gift? To me it feels like both an honor and an obligation. When I feel it descend—and you always know in advance that it's coming— I feel a duty to try and transcribe what I am given to the best of my ability. I scrabble around, I get away from other people, I need to find peace, a quiet space. I sneak off to the toilet if I have to, I find those scraps of paper and I ready myself.

Today though, sitting here, something suddenly came to me, a question, something to wonder about. I have always found this Muse to be insistent, strident even. It makes demands of me, I've felt, and I've been happy to meet them because I know that being chosen is something to take seriously, an honor to be quietly grateful for. But I wondered today: what if it isn't insistent, strident, demanding, this Muse? What if those are my projections, built from my own sense of obligation and a neurotic desire to please authority figures? What if, far from demanding, the Muse is gently asking? What if, rather than blaring at me from on high—*take this down now!*—she is instead standing quietly at my shoulder, offering me a gift with lowered gaze, extending her hands, shyly saying: *I made something for you. Would you like it...?*

I think that would change everything.

51.

I mean to say: this is an organic book. It has grown, piece by piece, stone by stone, like a vernacular cottage. It has no architect, or none that I know of. It was not plonked down. It emerged.

Our land has emerged the same way. When we came here we were full of plans. Jyoti and I were doing a distance-learning horticulture course. We had all sorts of ideas about mapping the land in great detail, planning out a permaculture garden, working out the planting and the rhythms in detail. In the end, we gave it all up, threw out the plans, stopped the course and just did what came, what seemed needed and wanted. Walk the land for long enough and you see where the sun sits and where the moss grows, where the natural paths are, where things want to grow, what is convenient, what is unlikely to work. You talk to other people, you get ideas, you see what the wildlife is doing and the garden, like the book, emerges from what is happening today, now, here. No one is in charge. The land, the garden, becomes a living response to an ever-roiling world, a green improvization under the sun. And better for it: so much better.

This knowing: it is real. If only I could turn my forebrain off, retune my rational mind, get back to the Garden always—then this place, this work, this being would be enough. It would be enough.

Another way of putting that: *everything would be all right, if only I could stop being human.*

52.

John Berger, another writer, another restless intellectual, though a real one rather than a pretend one like me, another literary urbanite who fled to the land to root himself in some older reality, once told his mother's ghost: 'I've always put life before writing.' This is the kind of person I thought I was until I got lost in this wood. Life before writing. Writing that serves life.

Not the other way around. That was what I thought I did. It was what I did. Maybe it is what I will do again. I don't know.

But all the time, at some level, I'd have to admit that writing has always felt more real to me than life. More real and more interesting. The patterns you can make from what you see out there are better than what you actually see out there, because they are yours. 'It is a life in itself,' wrote Lawrence, of the creating of his fictional worlds, 'far better than the vulgar thing people *call* life.' This is a catastrophically egotistical worldview and I expect I ought to feel ashamed about it, but I don't. What can I say in my defence? Not much. I think John Berger must have been a better man than I am. Or maybe he just had a better map.

His mother's ghost did reply. 'Don't boast,' she told him.

53.

It's not complicated, says Loki, cracking open another can of something cheap-looking. *It's life. It happens to the best. Here you are with all these roles you've taken on. Father, husband, smallholder farmer, provider, man of the community, writer with a social conscience, aspiring D. H. Lawrence. How does that all fit together? Where's the space for me in there? You need to throw it all off, mate. Crack it all open. Have a breakdown, or something. Breakdowns can be very productive when you're uptight. Do you know that when a caterpillar retreats into its chrysalis it actually dissolves? It doesn't just grow legs and wings—it reconstitutes itself at the molecular level. It becomes this gooey mess, and then emerges as something else. Nothing else will do when it's chrysalis time. No point in resisting. Dissolve your roles. Dissolve your reputation. Dissolve all your stories. It's the only way to find out what comes next for you. Of course, you've no idea what that is, any more than a caterpillar can imagine being a butterfly. Might be good, might be terrible. You might end up in the gutter. But that's what the gods are demanding of you now. Dissolution. Nothing less will do. Trust me, I asked them.*

Piss off, Loki, I reply, weakly. *Nobody believes a word you say.*

He grins.

Suit yourself, he says. *It's going to happen whether you go with it or not. It's just messier if you push against it. Have you got any more of these, by the way? Your fridge is empty.*

54.

I regret every word I have ever written, and every word I will ever write.

And I stand by all of it.

55.

I read somewhere that Roman Emperors, on their death beds, would receive a round of applause from the assembled worthies for the act they had played over their lives. It was like taking off a mask at the theatre and finally revealing their true face. *Well done*, the audience would signal. *Great acting!*

I don't remember where I read this. Is it true? I don't really care. It's such a good story, and that's always more important than whether it actually happened.

56.

Remember Russell Means? Here's another man of the Oglala Lakota, Black Elk, who told the story of his life and work to poet and ethnologist John Niehardt in the 1930s. Black Elk was a Holy Man, which meant he was also a healer. But he didn't heal alone:

> *I cured with the power that came through me. Of course, it was not I who cured, it was the power from the Outer World, the visions and the ceremonies had only made me like a hole through which the power could come to the two-leggeds.*
>
> *If I thought that I was doing it myself, the hole would close up and no power could come through. Then everything I could do would be foolish.*

Writers, when they get lucky, or pray at the right altars, are also a hole through which some power comes. Now I'm thinking again of the White Goddess, or the shy woman standing at my shoulder with offerings of words, and I'm thinking that if you were to change 'cured' to 'wrote' in that paragraph, then Black Elk and Robert Graves might have a lot to talk about, and that I would love to join the conversation, or at least stand in the corner and listen.

57

A few months back, I had to go to London. I had some interviews and some meetings and the kind of things you go to London to do. I arrived in the morning with some hours to fill, so I decided to visit the National Gallery. I hadn't been there for years, and it was free, which is always a consideration. Writers are not proud. Pictures, I thought, can be a good balm when there are too many words in your head.

I dropped my bag in the cloakroom and bought myself a map and headed for the rooms with the Turners and Gauguins and Van Goghs, distracted on the way by a series of vast Canaletto landscapes of the Grand Canal in Venice. I would like to live on the Grand Canal. I would like to drop all of this and move to Venice with Jyoti and change my name and wear a linen suit every day and wander the streets and drink strange orange drinks in little bars down crumbling alleyways and gaze up at huge Tintorettos in dark old churches, forever.

London. I had thought the gallery might take me to another place for a while, and it did, but not the one I expected. As I paced through its vast marble and gilt halls, weaving in and out of the other daytrippers, I felt a strange heaviness slip down over me, as if from the great stone domes above. Suddenly all this history, all these accretions of received image and overtold stories, seemed dark and oppressive. I wanted to throw off, to run from, all the accretions, from all the centuries of oiled portraits of doges, knights and electors, from the prophets with their snake sticks, from the black slaves holding platters and the white mistresses grimacing under broad hats, from the squires and the racehorses and the sailing ships and the endless nativities and crucifixions. All the weight of the past that was lying on me, and I hadn't even known what it had made me, and what did it have to do with me, any of this? Who said this was my history, my culture, who said I belonged to it? Nobody ever asked me, and yet I took it all on and suddenly, now, it was another weight to be sloughed off. The heavy ceilings and the dark wood, the ways of being laid under. Of course the artists and the writers wanted to crawl out from under this as soon as they got the chance, of course they wanted the weight to leave them, of course they spent the last century happily casting it all away and trampling it under. How else could they be free?

And in the gallery, under the dome, I found myself thinking: *I don't want to belong anymore. I don't want this weight anymore.*

I don't want to belong.

I want to *be*.

58.

Art: this is what I want more of in my life. I wish I knew something—anything—about art, beyond what I've picked up over the years just by seeing things I like and looking for more of the same. I wish I could walk knowledgeably around galleries and understand the history of Renaissance painting, the difference between a Caravaggio and a Titian, the cultural moment that the German landscape painters came from, the difference between Impressionism and Expressionism. I'd like to know everything about the history of art from the paintings on the wall of the Chauvet cave to the dawn of Modernism. I ought to buy myself a hefty illustrated book about Renaissance Italy. Maybe I could go on a course, do a Grand Tour of galleries and churches, maybe I could write about art instead of the death of the world. Yes! That's the thing. I will sit in pavement cafes in the Mediterranean sun and expound about Monet and Van Gogh. I will dream of what Paris was like before Europe began rotting in a stew of sugar and electricity. I will wear a broad brimmed hat and drink alcoholic things with vegetables in them. Words will appear from the high blue sky, like the sunflowers on the canvas.

Art, I suppose, in the broadest sense of the word, is the difference, if there is a difference, between writing fiction and writing non-fiction. Not that non-fiction can't be art—if you believe that, go and read some Annie Dillard—but in the writing of fiction, the creating of worlds, there is a freedom to dream and to be drawn that is not available if, as I am doing now, you are tethering your words to some version of externally accepted reality. Everything I am writing in this book is true, as far as it is ever possible to represent truth with words. Everything I am writing in this book is an attempt to strip something away and see what is underneath it, and that is also what fiction does at its best and what poetry has to do all the time.

But without that tethering to accepted reality, as Kundera points out, writing can soar and dive into places it could never otherwise go, as a Turner or a Van Gogh can, as all the best art does, as anything interesting at all will always do, and in doing so it will often excavate the depths of what it means to be human better than any fact ever can, because facts are the things that float on the surface of the boiling lake and we only take them so seriously because we can see them right here in front of us right now, and thus they seem more solid than what lurks down at the bottom by the hydrothermal vents, with seven blind eyes and a light on a stalk on its head, burping carbon dioxide into our psyches without us ever knowing it.

59.

'When I paint,' said Picasso, 'my object is to show what I have found and not what I am looking for.'

60.

In Martin Amis's short story "The Janitor on Mars," humanity is contacted by a source on the red planet and instructed to send a mission. When they arrive, they are met by the single surviving remnant of an ancient Martian master race—the Janitor. It turns out that he was programmed, millions of years ago, to make contact with the human race when their extinction was imminent—but only after it was too late to prevent it.

Before he breaks this news to them ('Oh come on. What did you expect? This is *Mars*, pal!') he has a question for them. He is puzzled by humanity's one distinguishing characteristic—their propensity for art. In every other area of endeavor, he explains, from science to politics, humankind has barely advanced beyond the level of pond slime. But the art is a different matter:

> *Art is not taken very seriously in this universe or in any other. Nobody's interested in art. They're interested in what everybody else is interested in: the superimposition of will. It may be that nobody's interested because nobody's any good at it. ... It's strange. Your scientists had no idea what to look for or where to look for it, but your poets, I sometimes felt, divined the universal...*

Why, the Janitor wants to know, has humankind been so dedicated to the creation of art, in all its many forms, from music to poetry to painting? He has a theory: that human history happened the way it did, with all of its horrors, in order that it might provoke the creation of great art:

> Like Guernica happened so Picasso could paint it. No Beethoven without Bonaparte. The First World War was to some extent staged for Wilfred Owen, among others. The events in Germany and Poland in the 1940s were set in motion for Primo Levi and Paul Celan. Etcetera. But I'm already getting the feeling it isn't like that...

'No, sir,' he is told, 'it isn't like that.'

'Well in a way,' he says, 'this makes my last chore easier.'

61.

I have a friend who is a green woodworker. He lives in the north of England, and I haven't seen him for years, but today I came across his website. He's been making ash splint baskets. I didn't know what an ash splint basket was until I saw the pictures but the beauty and the simplicity of his work struck me hard. To be able to make something like that: it seemed like a real skill, a real use of the hands, not like typing. I should make ash splint baskets, I thought. I should stop writing and make ash splint baskets until I can make one so beautiful that I never want to stop looking at it, because beauty is the thing, isn't it? Beauty is what gives life meaning, beauty is the light in the awesome dark, beauty is what we all want and need, it is life and without it we waste. To Robinson Jeffers, craggy old California poet, beauty was an objective external reality, something which existed outside of us, in 'the pristine granite' of the cliffs and mountains, not simply a product of human aesthetics. 'The beauty of things was born before eyes,' he wrote, 'and sufficient to itself; the heartbreaking beauty / Will remain when there is no heart to break for it.'

Is there a beautiful sentence in this book? Even one per book would make me happy. Those are my ash splint baskets. When I can make them I am proud, but they are never pleasing to the eye, only the ear and the mind, and they are never pleasing to the hands either. You can't live by typing and thinking, you can't live by pen and paper. Maybe you can't live by ash splint baskets either, but I know a real thing when I see one, and a beautiful thing too.

My woodworking friend wasn't always a woodworker. Once he was an academic scientist. He threw it all away to make ash splint baskets and scythe handles and greenwood spoons, and he's never looked back.

62.

When we planted our trees in the field this winter, we decided to put a wide circle of Scots pines right at the high point, where the field crowns a gentle rise before descending the hill. Scots pines are comical things in their first couple of years: tiny little stumps ringed with verdant green whiskers and rusty cones which look like baby rattles. They start small and grow slow and last longer than people. When I am old, if I am old, maybe I'll see them start to mature. I'd like that.

Last night I stood in the pine circle in the evening. A great tit was peeping somewhere, a wood pigeon calling, rooks cawing and passing overhead regularly, dominating the sky lanes. All the birds were preparing for sleep. Sometimes I feel the gauze split for a second, and it split now and I thought: *it is time to stop looking into the darkness*. I felt I'd been passed this information through the rift, though it felt not like information, really, but more like a quiet order: *stop, now*.

For 10 years I have been staring at the darkness without a shield. For 10 years, there has been a weight on me. I have tried to work with it. I have treated it like a duty, tried to help others with their weight too. But I realized at dusk, under the flight path of the rooks, that this weight on me was perhaps not words or my need to belong, but was the weight of knowing too much, seeing too much, taking on too much, staring too long into the abyss, taking it all so *personally*. Since my dad died, I have not torn my gaze away from it. Now, it feels like time

for some light

at last.

63.

I went out to the hazel wood, because a fire was in my head. By a stream in a clearing sat a woman in a red dress. She was tremendously beautiful.

I am so thirsty, she said. *Would you fetch me water?*

I have no water, I said. I don't know how I came here.

The stream, she said. *Use your imagination. You seem to think you have one.*

Who are you? I asked.

Freya, she replied. *Goddess of love, sorcery, birth, sex. War, death. It's all connected. We need to talk about Loki.*

OK, I said.

I suppose you know you can't trust him? she said. *He is a terrible liar. Once he accused me of sleeping with every god in Asgard. There are plenty I wouldn't touch with a krókspjót! Have you seen the state of Tyr? I'm not saying Loki will always lie, of course. Sometimes he can be very direct. And even a lie can communicate a truth. So it's not that he's wrong in what he says to you, necessarily. It's just that there might be stories he isn't telling you.*

What stories? I mumbled.

Well, that's for you to work out, she smiled. *That's where the fertility comes in, and the war. Maybe the sex, too. Loki wants chaos. That's what he comes for and what he brings. Sometimes you need chaos. Sometimes chaos is what keeps you alive, keeps you moving, running, burning. Sometimes chaos is what breaks you out of outmoded patterns. I'd only say that there are certain kinds of chaos, and then there are other kinds. You might want to think about the distinction.*

I will, I said, feeling like a small boy. She smiled again, and I wanted to stay there forever, and also I wanted to cry.

Now, she said. *The water?*

64.

In my 40th year, I took up Zen Buddhism. As a discipline, a practice, it sounds intimidatingly mystical, and its followers can sometimes enjoy making it seem more so, but its essence is the simplest—and therefore also the most challenging—thing on Earth. It's about paying attention. The most succinct description of Zen is also one of the most famous: *a finger pointing at the moon*. What would become Zen developed in China in the 5th century, as the teachings of the Buddha came in with wandering monks down the Silk Road from India and merged with indigenous Daoism to create a stark, stripped-down version of Buddhism, which itself is all about stripping everything back and paying attention to what remains.

Everything we experience, said the Buddha, is a product of the mind. Human life is a series of delusions—or stories—invented by the mind to explain the world of sensory experience, and the source of human unhappiness is our clinging to these delusions as if they were reality. Pay enough attention to the workings of your mind and you'll see the delusions being created. Once you can see them, they are more likely to drop away, or at least release their hold over you. I've always seen Zen as a kind of Buddhist puritanism. Strip away all the scriptures, the golden statues, the robes and bells and bowls and temples and what are you left with? The moon, and the finger. What is Zen? Its Japanese masters have a two-word answer: *just sitting*.

I was attracted to Zen because it seemed like a good way to prevent myself from going mad. Writers spend their whole lives in their minds, but often they don't understand how those minds work. That's not really part of the job. It doesn't matter where the story comes from as long as it comes, and if you try to understand where it comes from you might find that it stops coming. 'It's rather hard to be a good artist and also be able to explain intelligently what your art is about,' said the poet John Ashbery, understatedly. What he didn't add was: 'and it's dangerous to try.'

Zen, for me, is the antidote to the call of the wild gods with their demands, and the Muse with her offerings, and all of the pulling and tugging of the creative impulse, whatever it is. Every day, in theory at least, I sit silently on a stool for half an hour and I just watch what my mind does. I watch what obsesses it, I notice how thoughts trigger feelings, I see the paths it wends down. It calms me, if I'm lucky, because I can start to see how I work. And very occasionally, if I am luckier, I might get a glimpse of the experience the Zen masters call *kensho*: a tiny flash of the true nature of reality. The boundaries of everything will suddenly dissolve away, and that horrible New Age word *oneness* will make sense at last. Everything, it turns out, really is connected to everything else. If you're lucky, this insight might last a second or two, but you'll never forget it.

Kensho, though, as the Masters will tell you sternly if you mention it to them, is not the point of Zen. The point of Zen is that there is no point. Forget the *kensho*, they will say. Stop seeking. In the seeking is the pain. Just sit. *It is*, they will say, *what it is*.

If writing is undertaken in service to a god, or gods, then Zen is undertaken in service to nothing at all, or to everything, depending on your point of view. As such, I have hoped that perhaps it can save me from myself. Pay enough attention to who you think you are, and you find out soon enough what you are not. You will see that you are not your body, your ideas, your opinions, your history, your emotions, your thoughts. All of that stuff changes from year to year, from minute to minute.

You are not the person you were half an hour ago, let alone 10 years ago. So who are you? What essence remains? Is anything about you unchanging? Is anything about anything unchanging? If not, what does it even mean to talk about who 'you' are, what 'you' want, what 'you' think and feel?

Start to notice this—start to sit with it—and you will find, on a good day, that a strange calm descends, and you will find that it has saved your life.

65.

The problem with Zen is that it does tend to destroy you. That's really the point. I wonder if practicing it, albeit sporadically, for five years has been part of what is cracking me open now. 'Who am I?' is its fundamental question, and once you start asking it you find that the answer is… well, interesting.

To live is to suffer, said the Buddha, and the root cause of this suffering is craving—craving pleasure, craving pain, craving sex, power, food, attention, money, peace, excitement, enlightenment, anything. What is it that craves? It is your ego—your created sense of a permanent 'self'—and it craves because it believes that if it can have what it craves it will stop suffering. This is the story of our civilization, and we are discovering the hard way that it doesn't work. The pursuit of 'progress' or 'economic growth' or 'life, liberty, and the pursuit of happiness' are all cravings, all goals which, when reached, suddenly slip from our grasp, leaving behind oil spills and the stumps of forests. Satisfying your cravings doesn't work because the ego wants what it wants, regardless of the consequences for itself and for others, and it never knows when to stop.

We have built a whole society on what a Buddhist would say is a delusion—the primary delusion. The only way to end suffering, said the Buddha, is to end the cravings that create it, and that's where the hard work starts. It's a lifetime's work, the work of attention and self-knowledge, the hardest work, the work that none of us really wants to undertake.

Since I took up Zen, a question has stalked me: is writing an example of this craving, grasping, ego-self? Is the terrible, narcissistic ego of the self-identified 'writer' part of the same problem? When the self-centered delusions which keep the 'writer' attached to his career, his reviews, his reputation, his style, his back-catalog are ripped away, what is left? What is he writing for?

How would you write if you believed that you didn't really exist?

And is that the same question as, 'what god does my writing serve?'

66.

I began my Zen practice at the deep end, with a week-long silent retreat in an electricity-free farmhouse on a wet Welsh mountain. This is my idea of a week off. After a few days of trying to get into the whole thing and failing and becoming fed up and frustrated, I was sent out for a walk by the teacher. She could see that I was having trouble sitting still. Go for a walk she said, walk slowly, just pay attention to what you see. Don't judge it or think about it particularly, just let it be there. So I did. I saw a slug eating a mushroom in the dewdropped grass and I watched it for 15 minutes. Have you ever seen a slug eating? Just to pay attention to the small things breaks the carapace of your seeing, if only for a moment. I've had more appreciation for slugs ever since, though I still feed them to the chickens.

I walked slowly uphill for maybe a mile or so and I came across a fence. The mist had come down by now, a wet Welsh mountain mist and this fence snaked off into the mist in a line and disappeared into it. I stood by one of the fence posts and looked up the fence and then down the fence. In one direction, uphill, the next fence post had a metal cap on it. In the other direction, downhill, it was a standard wooden post, slightly rotten, barbed wire attached to it with metal staples. I looked up the fence again and down the fence again and the metal post was the future and the wooden post was the past, and I realized that I spent around 70 percent of the time in my head, living in one or the other, usually dreaming of the past and dreading the future. The post I was standing by, which represented the present, rarely got a look. I was never here.

I went back and told my teacher this, and she laughed her head off.

Sometimes I feel that time is an illusion, that I don't have a past, that the endless permutations of the process of always-becoming happen like everything else behind the gauze that separates me from reality. The fence stretches off and I can never really touch it. It might not even be real. It might be a story. The whole world is an illusion, a game, a freak show. There is no past, no future, no me, and therefore nothing to belong to. I don't have a past because nobody has a past, we are all living in some giant computer simulation or God is mocking us or God fled long ago or there is no God and no programmer and nothing but dark matter and the universe expanding out into... well, what? What could it possibly be expanding into?

67.

You take your craving and you lay it onto the place where you are, or onto the place you ran from or are running to, or the person. You write a story that says: *yes, it is all here for me, if only I can hold on to it.*

And then it all slips away, and you start again.

68.

As I grow older, the colors seem to become cleaner, simpler. A lot of effluvia flows away, things seem clarified somehow. I am 44 years old now. I am in the last half, the last third, the last quarter of my life; whichever it is, the active part, the burning, is behind me and dying back in time. The second half of a life is governed by the moon, not the sun. It is water time, not fire time, and I can no longer write books with plots that work, I can no longer structure stories and bring them to a climax, I can no longer craft and carve the paragraphs and the sentences. I can't plan a narrative journey because none of it makes sense to me now and if I think like that, if I think that that is the work, then I cannot even pick up a pen.

It's a terrible and a liberating discovery. Life is not that shape. Life is not the shape of a book.

69

What would happen, I wonder, if all writers were legally dis-
barred from writing about anything of which they didn't have
direct, personal experience? There would be far fewer books in
the world, for a start, which would probably be no bad thing, and
maybe those that remained would be tighter, smarter, and more
honest. Or maybe not. Maybe it's a terrible idea. Still, sometimes
I think I will write a book which aims at nothing, proves nothing, and does nothing: simply represents the world-as-it-is. This
book will just be a list of things I have directly experienced,
perhaps over a 24-hour period. 'A woman walks across a bridge.'
'A young birch in the April sun.' One long haiku, the most honest, if also the most boring, piece of literature ever written. But
of course it would still be as untrue as anything else painted in
words. All the experiences would still be filtered through this
creation named Paul Kingsnorth, who noticed the woman on
the bridge rather than red car which drove past at the same
time, and who thought that an April sun was sufficiently different from an October sun that to mention it might spark an image
in your mind, a feeling, a body-memory that might fleetingly join
your perception to mine and bring us together. I am a filter and
you are a filter and we are alone, trapped in our perceptions,
and we see different worlds. Scientists have been telling us for
years that our brains are perception-filters, that what we see of
the world is not 'reality' but simply what our brains make of it,
usually based on pattern recognition. We knew this even before
the scientific method could demonstrate it: Immanuel Kant was
telling us the same thing 250 years ago, apparently, though I'm
not going to pretend to have read *Critique of Pure Reason*.

In this context, words become bridges, reachings-out, from one
filter to another. Words become—writing becomes—a means

of confirmation. *Do you see the same world as me? You do? Then I am not alone!* Words can connect our worlds, and that's one reason, maybe, that we write them. But while words can join the filters together for a time, I think that nothing can dissolve the filters except the silence: except sitting and watching and listening and saying nothing. The author of the *Dao De Jing* knew this 2500 years back. 'He who knows does not speak,' he wrote. 'He who speaks does not know.' Every generation forgets this, I suppose, and the next one has to learn it again.

70.

In *The White Goddess*, Robert Graves tells us that all True Poetry throughout history is a variation on what he calls The Theme. This is 'the antique story, which falls into thirteen chapters and an epilogue, of the birth, life, death and resurrection of the God of the Waxing Year.' In case this is not definitive enough, Graves explains further that the central chapters of this tale must 'concern the God's losing battle with the God of the Waning Year for love of the capricious and all-powerful Threefold Goddess,' she of the hooked nose and rowan-berry lips.

We have lost touch with The Theme nowadays, says Graves—writing in 1948—because we are locked into the Machine, and the Machine is a demon which destroys both poetry and truth. This is the tragedy that has made both our poetry and our culture rotten:

> *'Nowadays' is a civilization in which the prime emblems of poetry are dishonoured. In which serpent, lion and eagle belong to the circus tent; ox, salmon and boar to the cannery; racehorse and greyhound to the betting ring; and*

*the sacred grove to the saw-mill. In which the Moon is
despised as a burned-out satellite of the Earth and woman
reckoned as 'auxiliary State personnel'. In which money
will buy almost anything but truth, and almost anyone but
the truth-possessed poet.*

Until poetry returns to its wild roots, there is no hope for civilization. Until civilization returns to its wild roots, there is no hope for poetry. To start this process, Graves blasted the Canon: the history of literature in Britain, he declared, should not begin with *The Canterbury Tales*, but with "Song of Amergin," an ancient Celtic calendar-alphabet which is the Great Spirit made word, the green fuse written down, the oral tradition pinned to the paper by symbols still living, still twitching:

> I am a stag: *of seven tines,*
> I am a flood: *across a plain,*
> I am a wind: *on a deep lake,*
> I am a tear: *the Sun lets fall,*
> I am a hawk: *above the cliff,*
> I am a thorn: *beneath the nail,*
> I am a wonder: *among flowers,*
> I am a wizard: *who but I*
> *Sets the cool head aflame with smoke?*

71.

Recently, at a conference in America, I watched Martin Shaw, my mythologist friend (everyone should have a mythologist friend), tell the story of *The Odyssey* over the course of a week to a crowd of 200 people. It was quite something. When you hear an accomplished oral storyteller tell a story, you are brought up hard against a fact that everyone in a pre-literate culture would have known from experience: a story is a living thing. When the storyteller begins, some strange animal lurches into the room, curls around the roof beams, intervenes, changes everything. A story is a summoning from the otherworld. And some tales want to have their way with you.

Stories live, especially when they are freed from the chains imposed on them by the written word. Even within those chains, there is freedom of movement. I have written two novels from the strange space of unknowing which grows around you when a story approaches and makes demands. I have had demands made of me by magical goldsmiths and pagan gods and black cats, and after a while you learn that there is nothing to do but open yourself up. There is nothing to do but be open.

When you hear an oral tale told well, you often find that a particular scene or image will lodge in your mind, and refuse to be shifted. There is usually a reason for this; you just have to discover it. As I heard *The Odyssey*, I found myself clinging, with Odysseus, to a piece of broken raft, after Poseidon the sea god has tried yet again to drown him. Poseidon does this a lot. Ino, a *nereid* of the ocean and no friend of Poseidon, sees Odysseus clinging to his broken vessel, and makes him an offer. She hands him a flimsy veil. I imagine it being multicolored, for some reason; rainbow silk. Take off your clothes, she says to him, and tie this around your body. Then let go of the raft. The veil will support you and take you to land.

Can Odysseus trust her? Should he let go of the raft, which provides him at least some small security in the storm? Will the veil save him or will he drown? He doesn't know. He has to answer a stark and impossible question: *do I trust this, or do I not?*

Everything I have clung to, for too long: I am sinking under it. Now I have to take the veil and strike out into the storm. It might drown me. But I've come far enough to trust this instinct, and to know at least one thing for certain: if I don't let go, I'm dead.

72.

You know your problem? shouts Loki, from the top of a storm-flecked wave the size of a tower block. *You're not curious enough!*

He shouts something else, something inaudible, through the lashing waters, then heaves a breath.

You know your other problem? he continues, almost screaming to be heard. *You actually believe in answers!*

73.

All year, especially in the spring, we are awakened at dawn by a wall of birdsong. This place is alive with the song of birds, more so each year as we plant more trees, encourage more insects, and allow them to build nests in all sorts of ridiculous places. It's so common, so wide and deep in the air and the land, that I'm in danger of taking it for granted.

This word—'birdsong'—is it accurate? Bird*song*? It sounds like singing to us, it sounds melodic and beautiful, or some of it, but this word has the wrong resonance, surely? *Song*, in human cultures at least, is something created for pleasure, for entertainment, for ritual, for worship. Song is beauty, creativity, religion, art, song is common to all human cultures but is also non-essential, beyond the everyday business of eating and hunting and working and shitting and sleeping.

But for a bird, what we have labeled *song* is a tool to be used for those essential things. The sounds being made by birds in the field at dawn, as far as humans can tell, are not the joyful melodies of creatures welcoming the beauty of the sunrise. They are birds seeking mates, warning off predators, warning each other of threats, staking out territory. They are conversations, perhaps, or boasts, or threats, or seductions. Some birdsong appears to be the equivalent of a human fencing in a piece of land and putting up a NO TRESPASSING sign. Sound is used to build a wall.

Last year, a single swallow roosted on a beam above our back door all summer. He covered our doormat in white and purple shit, but none of us minded. Jeevan christened him Fluffy, and wrote a story about him. When he left at the end of summer, we all missed him. Then, this April, he came back. From Africa, from southern Europe, from wherever he had been, he came back over thousands of miles of land and ocean and he found the same small beam and now he is back there, shitting on the mat again, sometimes balancing on the washing line or catching insects in mid-air. It's a small incredulity, and it lifts my heart.

You'll never see a swallow on the ground unless it's dead. If they come down to earth they find it hard to take off again. They are always on the move, but in cycles, in repeating patterns, like Yeatsian gyres. They belong to the movement and the patterns that they live on. Each evening, in the summer, Fluffy sits up on the electricity line above our back garden and he sings. Or rather, he makes an exhaustingly curious litany of sounds: chirrups, stutters, whistles, clucks, buzzes, always in the same order.

It's an amazing thing to hear. What does any of it mean? I have no idea. But he isn't 'singing.'

Birdsong is a story we have told ourselves, but it is not a story the birds tell. We tell stories about 'nature' all the time, and one of those stories is that there is something called 'nature' Out There, beyond the human, beyond 'civilization,' which is another story. 'Nature' is often somewhere we go to find peace: this is what it was for me for so long and still is. The green stillness. I can find great peace, great stillness, in my field, but the field is never still. Everything is busy. The grasses and the trees are photo-synthesizing, the insects are searching for nectar, the birds are nesting, chasing food, finding mates, fighting, the streams are ever-flowing, even the air currents are always moving. I come to places like this and sit here cross-legged and castigate myself for being so busy in my mind and in my body, load myself up with Puritan, or indeed Buddhist, guilt for not being still enough. But nothing else here is still. Everything is working all the time and if there is a difference between the grasses and the human who sits sometimes on the grasses, it is that the human doesn't just get on with his work, he *thinks* about getting on with his work.

She doesn't consider / what she was born to do, writes Mary Oliver of a turtle:

> *She's only filled*
> *with an old blind wish.*
> *It isn't even hers but came to her*
> *in the rain or the soft wind,*
> *which is a gate through which her life keeps walking.*

The human sitting here, the *me* perched on the grasses, con-stantly considers what he was born to do. He doesn't just do, he watches himself doing. He stands outside himself and is aware and can judge and his mind, the watcher, is his burden, it is the thorn which he carries with all of his kind, lodged deep in his flesh always. He can see himself and his work, he represents himself and his work in stories, he creates a language to hold them, and he writes it down.

Is language the trap? The field is full of language. Everything is speaking to everything else, and some of it I can hear and some of it, because of my biology or my cultural inheritance, I am not equipped to. All nature is a language—but none of it is written down. Writing: converting a living, dancing speech, a pattern of sounds from a pulsing animal body, to dead, unmoving symbols on a page. Writing: fossilizing life, replacing life with representations of life, representations which can be more attractive than life itself if you're not careful. Look: I have shown you my field. Probably you will never see it, and even if you do, you will not see what I see, because you are not me. All you have is my words, but my words are not my reality. I have nothing for you but black marks on white, which fire neurons in your brain. What if they fire the wrong neurons? What if I am setting off a chain reaction which will echo down the centuries and shade out reality, truth, with some bright white light?

If I read nothing for a year and if I wrote nothing for a year, would I, could I, begin to clear away the scaffolding which language, written language, conceptual, abstract language, has built up around my poor right brain? Could I fend off the assault which logic, reason, empiricism, analysis has been raining on my inner poet all my adult life? Could I silence the watcher? Could I split the gauze? Could I crawl out from under the barrage intact and begin to see what the world was before we remade it as a mechanism which could be taken apart and examined, before we measured the parts and sliced them up and fed them into the Machine? Before electric lights and asphalt and schooling and algorithms began to remake us? Could I please the gods that way? Could I burn my words like meat on an altar to appease them?

Would it be possible? I think I would give everything.

74.

Could I write like a tree would write, like a river would write, like an air current under a swallow's wing, the head of a plantain in the south of the field, a sycamore leaf falling to ground in early autumn? Could I sing the mathematics of it all in poems and watch them dance away and be lost beneath the umber loam? Could I write like a myth, like an intuition, like an animal hunting, a cloud skimming, could I write from the shores of the boiling lake, is there truth down there and can it ever be planted in symbols on a page?

It is what I have tried to do for years. But what if it is impossible? What if there can never be writing in these places, what if there are no written words on that shore, what if writing is their enemy, what if it shrivels them, burns them up like grass in a brown drought? What if writers are not welcome there

unless

So often, the very act of trying to write anything down, of trying to dissect it like a spavined insect, to lay it out on the white cloth ready for examination, kills the delicate thing I am trying to convey. The signifier cannot communicate the reality of the signified. The marks on the vellum are no longer the shapes of animals. The language dies and rots into the soil. Communication breaks down, misunderstandings happen, positions are taken, wars are started.

'We really ought to free ourselves,' implores Nietzsche, 'from the misleading significance of words!'

If you have never seen my field with the sun shining on it, if you have never lived inside me and I have never lived inside you, if we have never broken each other down in the spring air to see what the other is made of and then heard it well and carefully, then none of this can ever work. I can't ever know anything but what I see, feel, experience, and even then I can never *really* know it. I can only try to listen, to pay attention, to get myself out of its way as it speaks to me or at me.

I thought I wanted to belong, because I am lost. Remember that? I told you that a hundred pages ago and I haven't become any less lost since then, and that's fine. It's fine to be lost, though, just as it's fine to be quiet. It's necessary, sometimes. You don't start causing trouble unless your loss starts to burn the world around you, you don't start causing trouble unless you don't know that you are lost or why. If you do know, if you have paid attention—well then, you are just a seeker like everybody else and that's fine too, that's wonderful, in fact. And maybe sometimes in your seeking you will be granted a glimpse through the gauze, always uncalled for, always unexpected, often gone almost as it comes, but in the fragment of time you are given it, you will gasp then, and you will say:

Oh.

76.

My words have always served a purpose I set. They have always obeyed me. But my wizard's power is fading. My staff has been broken and my messianic tendencies, like Kavanagh's, are draining away. Messianic tendencies are such hard work. Suddenly, for the first time in my adult life, I have no agenda. I have words, but no master for them to serve. And I see now: I was never the master. I just thought I was.

'Creation is like anything else good,' said Charles Bukowski. 'You have to wait on it; ambition has killed more artists than indolence.' On his simple grave slab in the hard sun of California are engraved two words: *Don't try*.

77.

I thought I wanted to belong. I thought I needed to have a place, a people. But every time I find a place, I don't fit into it. Something takes me away from it, from the campfire to the slopes of the mountain. Every time I could belong, I push it away. So I suppose this must be who I am. Or, this must be one part of who I am, one faction, jostling with the others, Kavanagh wrestling with Yeats in mutual affection and resentment. I am lost, and is that what life is, what modernity or post-modernity is, a rolling sense of being out of place, of being tangled up in the gauze, of being alienated by language, perception, of having eaten the apple and fallen, and is *fall* another word for *life*?

Or are these just words? Just more words?

I like it here. Slowly, I am sinking into this place. As I regularly tell myself, I am lucky to be here, lucky to be alive here or anywhere, to be able to sit around and write books instead of worrying how to feed myself or escape a war. I don't want to leave—it would be another wrench—but I don't suppose this place will ever contain me or satisfy me, because who can ever be contained or satisfied? And why should this poor little plot of land have to bear the weight of meaning that some wandering primate has wanted to layer upon it? Why should anyone or anything have to bear the weight of our stories?

When I think about this word *belonging* I get tight in the chest. I build up narratives, I set boundaries and targets, theories and concepts begin to creep up on me from behind. The words which try to contain *belonging* are tight, clear, carefully punctuated, they move in order, one after another, like lines of soldier ants on dimpled leaves. But *being* can't be contained in any words at all. Being is freedom and responsibility all in one, and as hard as either, as impossible and easy. Maybe I could *be* here but not *belong* here, or maybe I will belong here in time, or maybe that's not my decision to make, or maybe, maybe, it doesn't matter at all because these are all symbols I arrange in my head while the world goes on around me and I wander the garden, chattering and buzzing like the swallow on the line, trying to get my story straight. And everything else is just getting on with things. Everything else is just busy.

Something calls me again: *Be quiet now. Be quiet.*

78.

At midsummer in the west of Ireland, the sky is never really dark. Night doesn't fall until nearly midnight and dawn takes hours to spread across the wide sky. Whenever you wake, it is light.

It is the middle of June as this book stumbles to its close, a few days out from the solstice. I am awoken at 5 a.m. by a sound at the window. A tap-tap-tap on the glass. I rise and go out into the garden. Loki is sitting on the bird table, swinging his legs.

Message from Mercury for you, he says.

Mercury's a Roman God, I say. You're Norse. How does this work, exactly?

It's the 21st century, my friend, he says. *We're all multicultural now. Listen, the gods have a deal for you. An offer. You want to hear it?*

No, I say, but I suppose you'll tell me.

Simple deal, he says, breaking open the bird feeder and picking at the peanuts. *They'll let you live a bit longer if you promise to shut up.*

Shut up? I say.

Just for a while, he says. *Maybe. I mean, could be forever I suppose. I didn't inquire about the time limit. But yeah, shut up. Stop writing. Stop talking. Just be. Let the silence in. Let go of all your ideas, all the structures you built, all the stories you have. They're blocking everything. If you want the words back, you have to give them a space to play in. Be attractive to them. Have some style. Stop pushing them around. Let them run free in the field. Dissolve like that caterpillar. Let go of the raft. Poseidon has promised to behave himself if you do, though I'd never trust a sea god myself. Brooding, they are, like the ocean.*

I suppose I've known about this offer for a while, I say. On some level, you know?

Of course you have, he says. *For the last forty thousand words at least. But you know what you're like. Things have to be written down before you believe they're real.*

He picks another peanut out of the feeder and examines it like a jeweler with a loupe in his eye and a strange brown pearl between his fingers.

So, he says. *What's your answer?*

79.

I wondered how to end this book, this book that I never really planned to start. The important thing was always going to be avoiding conclusions. I have always come to conclusions. I have always wanted to tie things up, lay them out cleanly, send you away happy or inspired or at least not too confused, not too let down. Now I need to leave all the threads loose and hanging. It is not my job to tie them, it is not anybody's job because they are not to be tied this time. There is nothing that can contain this, and conclusions are lies, cop-outs, offerings of weak comfort. For a while I thought maybe that if I just ended the book suddenly, just stopped somewhere, maybe even in the middle of a sen

No, it isn't going to work.

So let me just say what I need to say, whatever that turns out to be.

The old folk tales of Europe are full of men and women being dragged through the mire towards something new and necessary—wisdom? truth?—but they pay for it. They are consumed, they die and are reborn, they are flayed and tortured for small errors. The witches come to the court and drag them by their hair into the black forest, and if they emerge alive they are marked. The woman has three strands of grey hair, the man has a limp, and these things will never leave them. They have old eyes in young faces, now. Something has been sacrificed to pay for what they have seen. They have not bought their revelation cheaply, and neither can we.

The Zen nun meditates in a cave for 12 years, and when she comes down from the mountain she says, *everything is just as it was when I left*, and she says, *everything is changed*.

The women go into the river. The men go out to the bush.

Things come at you and break you, other things inhabit and form you. Words descend to help you explain, and sometimes they even manage it.

Some things remain inexplicable, now and forever.

I am being split apart in the sun. I don't know what will be exposed. Maybe nothing. Maybe there is nothing there and never was. Maybe I am deluded. I have been deluded many times.

But I understand the deal. It seems cruel. I suppose cruelty is as necessary as summer.

I want to see ahead, to try to understand where I am going, to direct myself. But in the dark wood, what looks like a path is as likely to be a dead end. I am no wizard.

Not this time.

Right now, lost in the undergrowth, I don't know anything. Who I am, where I am going, where I will end up, what I will do or should. I know none of it, and that's all I can see and come to. It's kind of wonderful. To be empty of all certainty, to have no answers, no wagons circled, no theories and no promises. I'm not sure I've ever been here before.

This is not a conclusion. Nothing is being contained here. I don't have a message, a comfortable ending to this uncomfortable book, a series of bullet-pointed calls for action. I have nothing to sell you. I have no conclusion, but I do have a suspicion. I suspect that all the paths out of the wood lead to the same place and all of the questions are the same question, and I can never shut up about anything and so, again, though I tried so hard not to, again I have written it all down. And here it is. And I offer it up to you. It is all I have.

Everything is questions, questions only now. Can I make myself quiet in a world that wants me to shout? Who will drag me through the cold river? Which path leads out of the wood? How can I make myself hear? How can I get out of my own way? If I do, when I do, what will be waiting beneath?

I ask: what must I do now?

And I wonder: what is the sacrifice?

But even as I ask,

I know the answer.

ACKNOWLEDGEMENTS

This was not an easy book to bring to fruition, and I owe gratitude to those who helped birth it. My agent Jessica Woollard believed in it when many others doubted, and kept me believing in it too. My friends Martin Shaw, Charles Foster, Jay Griffiths, Mark Lynas, Caroline Ross and Dougald Hine read various versions of the manuscript and offered their advice. Eric Obenauf and Eliza Wood-Obenauf at Two Dollar Radio took a punt on these pages when others passed.

But most of all I am grateful to my family, especially my mum and my wife Jyoti, who have allowed me to write about them and the life they have both shared with me, without throwing me out of the house or refusing to return my calls. A book like this is a kind of ripping-open; delicate surgery which carries a high risk of failure. It is impossible—of course—to find the right words to acknowledge this kind of love.

Two Dollar Radio
Books too loud to Ignore

ALSO AVAILABLE Here are some other titles you might want to dig into.

AT THE EDGE OF THE WOODS
NOVEL BY **KATHRYN BROMWICH**

← "Bromwich paints Laura and her woods as vibrantly as an old-fashioned fairy tale and this is just as foreboding. Fans of highly interiorized, richly narrated feminist fiction will tear through it." —Annie Bostrom, *Booklist*

HAUNTING, GORGEOUSLY DESCRIPTIVE, AND spellbinding, this is a magnificent and assured debut novel that delivers all the resonance and significance of an instant classic.

SOME OF US ARE VERY HUNGRY NOW
ESSAYS BY **ANDRE PERRY**

← "A complete, deep, satisfying read." —Gabino Iglesias, NPR

ANDRE PERRY'S DEBUT COLLECTION of personal essays travels from Washington DC to Iowa City to Hong Kong in search of both individual and national identity while displaying tenderness and a disarming honesty.

TRIANGULUM NOVEL BY **MASANDE NTSHANGA**

← "Magnificently disorienting and meticulously constructed, *Triangulum* couples an urgent subtext with an unceasing sense of mystery. This is a thought-provoking dream of a novel, situated within thought-provoking contexts both fictional and historical." —Tobias Carroll, Tor.com

AN AMBITIOUS, OFTEN PHILOSOPHICAL AND GENRE-BENDING NOVEL that covers a period of over 40 years in South Africa's recent past and near future.

THE WORD FOR WOMAN IS WILDERNESS
NOVEL BY **ABI ANDREWS**

← "Unlike any published work I have read, in ways that are beguiling, audacious…" —Sarah Moss, *The Guardian*

THIS IS A NEW KIND OF NATURE WRITING — one that crosses fiction with science writing and puts gender politics at the center of the landscape.

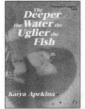

THE DEEPER THE WATER THE UGLIER THE FISH NOVEL BY **KATYA APEKINA**

→ 2018 *Los Angeles Times* Book Prize Finalist
← "Brilliantly structured… refreshingly original, and the writing is nothing short of gorgeous. It's a stunningly accomplished book." —Michael Schaub, NPR

POWERFULLY CAPTURES THE QUIET TORMENT of two sisters craving the attention of a parent they can't, and shouldn't, have to themselves.

NIGHT ROOMS ESSAYS BY **GINA NUTT**

→ **"A Best Book of 2021" —NPR**
→ **2021 Foreword INDIES, Finalist**
→ **2022 IPPY MEDALISTS for Essay, bronze**

← "In writing both revelatory and intimate, Nutt probes the most frightening aspects of life in such a way that she manages to shed light and offer understanding even about those things that lurk in the deepest and darkest of shadows."
—Kristin Iversen, *Refinery29*

THE UNDERNEATH NOVEL BY **MELANIE FINN**

← "A musk of sex and menace soaks three narrative strands, expertly braided." —*Kirkus Reviews*, starred
← "The prose is so dark it's practically burnt!"
—Molly Young, *New York Times*

THE UNDERNEATH IS AN INTELLIGENT and considerate exploration of violence—both personal and social—and whether violence may ever be justified.

BORN INTO THIS
STORIES BY **ADAM THOMPSON**

→ **The Story Prize Spotlight Award, Winner.**
→ **Readings Prize for New Australian Fiction, Shortlist.**
→ **Age Book of the Year award, Finalist.**
← "With its wit, intelligence and restless exploration of the parameters of race and place, Thompson's debut collection is a welcome addition to the canon of Indigenous Australian writers." —Thuy On, *The Guardian*

THEY CAN'T KILL US UNTIL THEY KILL US ESSAYS BY **HANIF ABDURRAQIB**

→ **Best Books 2017:** NPR, *Buzzfeed, Paste Magazine, Esquire, Chicago Tribune, Vol. 1 Brooklyn,* CBC (Canada), *Stereogum, National Post* (Canada), *Entropy, Heavy, Book Riot, Chicago Review of Books* (November), *The Los Angeles Review, Michigan Daily*

← "Funny, painful, precise, desperate, and loving throughout. Not a day has sounded the same since I read him."
—Greil Marcus, *Village Voice*

WHITE DIALOGUES STORIES **BENNETT SIMS**

← "Anyone who admires such pyrotechnics of language will find 21st-century echoes of Edgar Allan Poe in Sims' portraits of paranoia and delusion, with their zodiacal narrowing and the maddening tungsten spin of their narratives."
— Hannah Pittard, *New York Times Book Review*

IN THESE ELEVEN STORIES, Sims moves from slow-burn psychological horror to playful comedy, bringing us into the minds of people who are haunted by their environments, obsessions, and doubts.

Books to read!

Now available at **TWODOLLARRADIO.com** or your favorite bookseller.

ALLIGATOR STORIES BY DIMA ALZAYAT

→ PEN/Robert W. Bingham Award, Finalist.
→ Swansea University Dylan Thomas Prize 2021, Finalist.
→ James Tait Black Memorial Prize, Finalist.
→ Short Story Prize, Longlist.
→ Arab American Book Awards, Honorable Mention.

← "The richly detailed short fictions in this debut from a Damascus-born scribe form an intricate, breathtaking mosaic of modern Muslim life." —Michelle Hart, *O, The Oprah Magazine*

FOUND AUDIO NOVEL BY N.J. CAMPBELL

← "[A] mysterious work of metafiction... dizzying, arresting and defiantly bold." —*Chicago Tribune*

← "This strange little book, full of momentum, intrigue, and weighty ideas to mull over, is a bona fide literary page-turner." —*Publishers Weekly*, "Best Summer Books, 2017"

THE BOOK OF X NOVEL BY SARAH ROSE ETTER

← "Etter brilliantly, viciously lays bare what it means to be a woman in the world, what it means to hurt, to need, to want, so much it consumes everything." —Roxane Gay

"A powerful novel." — Bradley Babendir, *Star-Tribune*

A SURREAL EXPLORATION OF ONE WOMAN'S LIFE and death against a landscape of meat, office desks, and bad men.

THE DROP EDGE OF YONDER
NOVEL BY RUDOLPH WURLITZER

← "One of the most interesting voices in American fiction." —*Rolling Stone*

AN EPIC ADVENTURE that explores the truth and temptations of the American myth, revealing one of America's most transcendant writers at the top of his form.

THE VINE THAT ATE THE SOUTH
NOVEL BY J.D. WILKES

← "Undeniably one of the smartest, most original Southern Gothic novels to come along in years." — Michael Schaub, NPR

WITH THE ENERGY AND UNIQUE VISION that established him as a celebrated musician, Wilkes here is an accomplished storyteller on a Homeric voyage that strikes at the heart of American mythology.